THE ART OF COUNTERPOINT

Second Edition

Da Capo Press Music Reprint Series

ROLAND JACKSON

GENERAL EDITOR

THE ART OF
COUNTERPOINT

by

C. H. Kitson

DA CAPO PRESS • NEW YORK • 1975

Library of Congress Cataloging in Publication Data

Kitson, Charles Herbert, 1874-1944.
  The art of counterpoint.

  (Da Capo Press music reprint series)
  Reprint of the 1924 ed. published by Oxford University
Press, London, New York.
  1. Counterpoint. I. Title.
MT55.K69A7 1975   781.4'2   75-4973
ISBN 0-306-70668-7

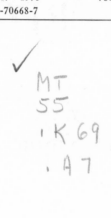

Published by Da Capo Press, Inc.
A Subsidiary of Plenum Publishing Corporation
227 West 17th Street, New York, N.Y. 10011

THE ART OF
COUNTERPOINT

BY

C. H. KITSON

M.A. (Cantab.), D.Mus. (Oxon.),
F.R.C.O. (Honoris Causa)
Professor of Music in the University of Dublin

SECOND EDITION

OXFORD
AT THE CLARENDON PRESS

London   Edinburgh   Glasgow   Copenhagen
New York   Toronto   Melbourne   Cape Town
Bombay   Calcutta   Madras   Shanghai
OXFORD UNIVERSITY PRESS
Humphrey Milford
1924

Printed in England

DEDICATED TO

HUGH PERCY ALLEN

M.A., D.MUS. OXON.

PREFACE

TO THE SECOND EDITION

THE first edition of this treatise was published in 1907. During the fifteen years that have elapsed, a considerable change has come over the outlook upon contrapuntal study in this country. This welcome change enables me in the second edition to carry to its logical conclusion what I had in mind in 1907, but felt at the time to be inopportune. If the technique of strict Counterpoint be deduced from the practice of the sixteenth century, it is only logical to employ the scalic system of that period. Fux used the modal system, and it should be restored. The atmosphere of sixteenth-century music cannot be obtained without using the modes. Further than that the technique is bound up with the modes, so that if the modern scales be employed, all sorts of difficulties in reference to unessential notes and harmonic progression arise, leading to all sorts of false conclusions.

Those who modernized strict Counterpoint evidently thought they were doing a real service in making it do duty as a kind of abstract technical study. But the result was that it taught neither sixteenth-century technique, nor any other.

In coming to the definite conclusion that strict Counter-point should be modal, there arose the question of the omission of the examples of the first edition, which are all written in the major and minor keys. A large number of new examples have been written in the modes: but a fair proportion of the original examples have been retained for two chief reasons. Firstly, students can compare the two schemes, and see clearly the differences between them. Secondly, strict Counterpoint with the modern scalic system is still required, and this book is thus serviceable for either purpose. Further it seemed hardly worth while to write new elaborate examples in from six to eight parts: and the major scale is after all one of the modes, though a much despised one.

Following this point of view to its logical issue, other changes are necessary.

(a) The principles of the period as to consecutives should be restored and permitted, if not always employed. The fact that they are not absolute is no argument against them: on the contrary the fact of their being characteristic of the period is a valid reason for their employment.

(b) In the period harmonic progression was calculated by a principle of intervals. The modern theory of chords was unknown. This principle simplifies and elucidates the formation of harmony, besides eliminating difficulties as to the use of unessential notes which belong to a later period and preventing confusion as to available resource. Further, in the course of experience, shorter and clearer ways of stating various points must become apparent; and as ideas as to strict Counterpoint become more enlightened, polemics become unnecessary. Thus important modifications will be found in Part I of this treatise under the above headings. There can be no argument about a point if it is substantiated by the period under discussion. The only point for argument is as to whether the period be accepted as the standard or not. If theorists do not accept it, it is for them to show from what other period they deduce their principles.

The latter half of this treatise in its original form dealt in a broad way with modern contrapuntal technique. It gave examples of the technique, but provided no means of obtaining it. Modernized strict Counterpoint was supposed to suffice, and we allowed our students to form their free technique in a haphazard way, chiefly by writing fugues, inventions, and choral preludes. Progress in this work has been hampered by insufficient technique, and Part II of this book is an attempt to provide it in as systematized a way as that of Part I. All the important examples of the original edition have been retained as illustrations of this technique: and it is hoped that the book in its new form will prove to be of increased usefulness.

C. H. KITSON.

London,
1924.

CONTENTS

PART I

SIXTEENTH-CENTURY COUNTERPOINT

CHAP.		PAGE
I.	Preliminaries	1
II.	First Species in two Parts	16
III.	Second Species in two Parts	30
IV.	Third Species in two Parts	46
V.	Fourth Species in two Parts	67
VI.	Fifth Species in two Parts	77
VII.	Counterpoint in Triple Time	89
VIII.	Counterpoint in three Parts	96
IX.	The First and Second Species in one of three Parts	101
X.	The Third Species in one of three Parts .	111
XI.	The Fourth and Fifth Species in one of three Parts	114
XII.	Combined Counterpoint in three Parts. .	122
XIII.	Counterpoint in four Parts	166
XIV.	Counterpoint in five Parts	194
XV.	Counterpoint in six, seven, and eight Parts	203
XVI.	The English School of the Sixteenth Century	226

PART II

MODERN COUNTERPOINT

CHAP.   PAGE

  I. PRELIMINARIES 235

  II. FIRST SPECIES 238

  III. SECOND SPECIES 248

  IV. THIRD SPECIES 255

  V. FOURTH SPECIES 263

  VI. FIFTH SPECIES 268

  VII. COMBINED COUNTERPOINT: FIRST, SECOND, AND THIRD SPECIES 273

  VIII. TWO PARTS IN SECOND OR THIRD SPECIES . . 284

  IX. FIRST, SECOND, AND FOURTH SPECIES, AND TWO PARTS IN FOURTH SPECIES 288

  X. THE REMAINING COMBINATIONS 293

  XI. COMBINED COUNTERPOINT WITH THE UNIFORM C. F. ELIMINATED 299

  XII. VARIOUS TYPES OF VOCAL COUNTERPOINT . . 319

  XIII. VARIOUS TYPES OF INSTRUMENTAL COUNTERPOINT 330

PART I

SIXTEENTH-CENTURY COUNTERPOINT

CHAPTER I

PRELIMINARIES

THE history of the art of Music up to the end of the nineteenth century falls into three main divisions:

A. In the first period, represented chiefly by the music of the ancient Greeks, the expression of the emotions in terms of formulated sound, consisted of a succession of single utterances called Melody.

B. The next stage is that in which men began to experiment in the possibilities of combined sound. There were two lines of procedure:

1. That of adding a part to a given part, called in Scholastic Counterpoint the Cantus Firmus, or Fixed Song.

2. That of forcing totally different melodies to be set one against the other.

The latter method was probably due to the fact that men found the task of adding three or more parts to a Cantus Firmus (C.F.), so as to produce euphonious combinations, so overwhelming, that out of sheer despair, or lack of the power of concentration, they selected a course which left such considerations to chance. Such a system, however, served the purpose of bringing before men's minds the effect of various harmonic intervals, and so helped them to form, in the process of time, a judicious selection of consonances.

It is true that among the Greeks there were signs of advance in the direction of combined sound. They perceived that the voices of men and children might be used to sing the same melody together at the distance of an octave; this they called Antiphony. But no progress could be made towards Polyphony, or the independent conception of parts, until men had

B

found out other consonances. The *Musica Enchiriadis* of Odo,
and the commentary upon it, called *Scholia Enchiriadis*, in-
augurated this principle, as distinguished from the old Greek
Antiphony, which was technically called Magadizing. It no
doubt had its origin in the fact that when several men were
singing the same melody together, some found it too high,
others too low; and the distance of an octave usually caused
difficulties at the other extreme. For reasons which need not
be here detailed, the intervals of the fourth and fifth were the
first to be selected as consonances :

In the earliest attempts, men made their voices move in
fourths or fifths in strict parallels. Sometimes, for technical
reasons, the added part held the same note for a time, until
it could proceed in parallel movement with the original part.

The fixed part was called the Principalis, and the added
part the Organalis. This system was known as Diaphony or
Organum. Odo's work belongs to the first half of the tenth
century. The next work of which we know, dealing with the art
of Diaphony, is the *Micrologus* of Guido d' Arezzo, written
in the first half of the eleventh century. Here we see a freer
sort of Diaphony, which admitted of sounds that had formerly
been held as discordant ; and also the use of oblique motion
as a means of variety, as opposed to its adoption from technical
reasons, in the older Diaphony.

Then, after the death of Guido (*circa* 1050) came a new
Organum, in which the use of contrary motion and the inter-
change of concord with discord became characteristic features.

Finally, the constant use of combinations in which the
Organalis was contrasted with the Principalis, not only in
melodic curve, but also in time value, led to the formation of
a system of musical standard of measure, called Discant or
Cantus Mensurabilis. Discant in its turn merged into Counterpoint. During all these periods a process of elimination in
reference to the selection of consonances resulted in the sur-

vival of the fittest, that is, those harmonic intervals which pleased
the ear best. These were the third, fifth, sixth, and octave :

The fourth was discarded owing to experiments in three parts
proving it to be unsatisfactory.

The Polyphonic Period may be said to close with the death
of Palestrina (1594). In him is seen the perfection of the
method ; and the technique of Counterpoint, as exhibited in
his works, is the subject of the first part of this treatise.

It is reasonable to inquire why Palestrina's work is taken as the
standard authority in preference to, for example, the work of our
own Byrd. The answer is that whereas Byrd shows the spirit of
adventure and enterprise—and this is true of the English School
as a whole—Palestrina is not an innovator. He was content
to apply the principles as he knew them. It is not that Byrd's
work is inferior—in fact it may be said to be superior in many
respects—but the student primarily requires to know precisely
what the principles are, and then to learn how to apply them.
A special chapter will, however, be devoted to the English School.

The work of Palestrina exhibited not only the high-water mark
in the independence of the separate parts and complexity of the
whole, as for example, in the Sanctus of the Missa Brevis or in
the following madrigal :

but also at other times a studied simplicity, in which, although the separate parts are still conceived as individual melodies, the effect is that of blocks of combined sound.

The following is the opening of his *Stabat Mater*:

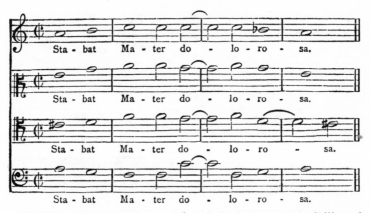

Sta - bat Ma - ter do - lo - ro - sa.

C. This brought before men's minds a greater possibility of beauty in combined melodies, by regarding the resultant sound vertically, that is, as blocks of harmony. And so the third or Harmonic Period was the natural evolution of the second. It may be said to begin with the dawn of the seventeenth century, and found its first culmination in J. S. Bach.

In the Polyphonic Period, the resultant harmony was the accident of the part writing. But in much of the work of Palestrina, the effect is very often that the whole is based on a simple harmonic structure; this was of course due to the awakening harmonic instinct and natural judgement as to the fitness of things. Under modern conditions, the horizontal movement is entirely built up from a preconceived harmonic basis.

The following is an illustration:

Fuga **VII.** *Das Wohltemperirte Clavier.* J. S. Bach.
à 3.

Harmonic Sub-structure.

Motives.

At first men were so much engaged with this vertical aspect of things, that they entirely ignored any questions dealing with the intrinsic merit of the individual parts.

The secularization of music, and the necessity of writing for instruments, tended at the outset to turn men's minds away from contrapuntal methods. They had to give their attention to the formation of melodies, in which rhythm was a characteristic feature ; and they had also to supply simple accompaniments to such melodies. Moreover polyphonic methods, which were entirely choral, were unsuited to a true instrumental style, and so the whole trend of things led to the enlargement of harmonic resource, and the formation of melody built upon such a substructure. All this progress was summed up in J. S. Bach, who adapted the principles of Harmony to Polyphony, and thus struck a just balance between the two.   The technique of Counterpoint in the Homophonic Period is discussed in Part II of this treatise.

It was only in the ordinary course of things, that when the art of Polyphony had come to maturity, theorists should devise a concise means of cataloguing its technique.   The salient feature of Counterpoint is the independent conception of the parts, not only in melodic curve, but also in time value ; so that it was only natural that Zacconi in his *Prattica da Musica*, published at Venice in 1596, should devise a means of considering complex movement under well defined heads.   He used a C.F. consisting of notes of uniform length; to this a part had to be added in notes of the same time value, or in certain classified contrasted values, such as two notes to one, four to one, and so forth ; these various ways of adding a part to a given C.F. are called Species or Orders, and Fux analysed the technique under five headings, called the Five Species of Counterpoint.   This was not by any means an exhaustive analysis of the technique of the art ; Zacconi wrote examples of Species which have not survived.   But the classification as settled by Fux has been maintained to the present day, and it is adequate for its purpose.

There are then four chief questions in reference to this technique :

1. What are the various sorts of complex movement arising from the independent conception of the parts ?

2. What are the rules of vertical combination under these separate conditions ?

3. What considerations regulate the melodic idiom of the parts ?

4. What was the scalic system ?

The scope of the investigation may be seen by referring to the opening bars of the madrigal quoted on p. 3.

(a) At the second half of the second bar the parts move simultaneously.   This is an example of First Species.

(b) At the second half of bar four there is an example of the movement two notes to one, termed Second Species.

(*c*) At the first half of bar two there are four notes to one—Third Species.

(*d*) At the end of bar eight there is Syncopation in the Tenor—Fourth Species.

(*e*) In bar seven the Alto and Tenor use florid idioms, or Fifth Species.

(*f*) At the first half of bar six there is a combination of First, Second, and Third Species : and at the latter half, First, Second, and Fourth Species.

In actual composition no species or combination of species is ever used consistently for any length of time, but in technical work it is necessary to concentrate on one thing at a time. So just as in harmony one sort of chord is taught at a time, so in Counterpoint we learn one sort of movement at a time : the former is vertical in aspect, the latter horizontal.

Next, there must be laws regulating the combination of parts, else the result would be mere cacophony. What intervals may be struck together, and what are the conditions which cause variety of procedure ?

For example, at the second minim of bar six the Tenor and Bass strike a sixth. What are the possibilities and limitations in such a case ? There is also the question of the treatment of discords in oblique movement as in bars two and three. Thirdly, the Alto in bar seven has a dotted minim, followed by two quavers ; it will be found a general practice of the period to use quavers only on the second halves of accents, and to approach and quit them by step. In bar eight the Tenor has two crotchets on the strong accent followed by a syncopated minim (written as a semibreve). This is also a convention of the period, though there are exceptions.

In the application of this technique the questions of rhythm and accentuation must be considered. For sixteenth-century methods were quite different from ours. The whole matter is discussed in Dr. Fellowes's *The English Madrigal Composers* (Oxford Press), to which the student is referred.[1]

---

[1] Also R. O. Morris, *Contrapuntal Technique*, recently published.

The rules governing the employment of the various species singly, and in combination, will be given under the separate groupings. But the fourth main question, the scalic system, must be briefly outlined here. If reference be made once more to the opening of the madrigal quoted on p. 3, and if the ending be examined:

PALESTRINA.

it will be seen that there is the key signature of one flat. But the music at the beginning sounds to our ears vague in tonality and at the end seems to be in B flat major, before closing in G minor with the Tierce de Picardie. It need hardly be said that this madrigal is in the Dorian Mode transposed. And as sixteenth-century technique is bound up with the ecclesiastical modes, the only logical thing to do is to employ the modes in learning it. If this is not done, there will be a hopeless confusion of principles, and a great deal that is characteristic of the period would have to be omitted. For example, both the following can only be explained under modal conditions:

BEVIN.   BYRD.

They do not belong to the modern scalic system. But the technique must be taken as it is found 'in toto', and questions referable to the modern scales must not be allowed to have weight in considering sixteenth-century technique. As a matter of fact this confusion of schemes has caused a very common error as to the precise meaning of Strict Counterpoint or strict style. The designation 'strict' is an unfortunate one as it implies disciplinary restrictions, whereas the term is really used to define the technique of the sixteenth century. The only reason for calling it strict is that as the history of the evolution of resource is the history of the infraction of rule, and expansion of principle, the rules and principles of this period are relatively inelastic. In the various attempts to make sixteenth-century technique serve for more modern conditions, there are serious departures from original practice in three main directions: (a) an enlargement of melodic idiom, (b) a restriction of 'harmonic' resource that never had any *locus standi*, (c) various restrictions in the laws of part-writing. There are only three valid reasons for restrictions in technique: (1) that the procedure is unmusical, (2) that it is faulty in style or taste, (3) that it is not a part of the technique of the period under consideration. All sixteenth-century polyphonic music is Strict Counterpoint, whether it be complex, as in the madrigal quoted on page 3, or simple as in the opening of the Stabat Mater (p. 5). All Counterpoint of the later harmonic periods is Free. Some authorities object to the term Free Counterpoint, on the grounds that all music of the Polyphonic Period is generically termed Counterpoint, and all music of later periods Harmony, being based on a principle of chords. Thus Free Counterpoint is merely another name for Modern Composition in which all the parts are individual and of equal importance. The quibble, however, is of no significance: but the student must understand that under modern conditions there are two distinct styles: (1) Harmonic, in which the parts harmonize a tune, or accompany it in harmonic style, as for example the familiar hymn tune, or song with arpeggio accompaniment; (2) Contrapuntal, in which all the parts are of equal importance, as in the fugue. Or the student may compare the Chorale harmonizations in Bach's *St. Matthew Passion* with his Choral Preludes for the Organ. Some one may say, why go so far back as the sixteenth century for study? There are many reasons. Three will suffice: (*a*) the music represents the zenith of pure choral contrapuntal writing in a period when the whole outlook was horizontal; (*b*) the harmonic resource is very slender, and the accident of the part-writing, so that the student is not worried by two problems at the same time; (*c*) the more we study the actual music of the period, the more we see what we have lost by allowing its characteristic features to fall into oblivion.

It remains then in this preliminary chapter to get a general idea of the use of the modes. They are as follows:

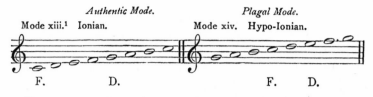

The first note of each Authentic Mode is called its Final (F.) and the C.F. always ends on this note, preceded by the note above it. Each Authentic Mode is regarded as a pentachord (or series of five consecutive white notes) with a tetrachord (or series of four consecutive white notes) above it. Thus in the Dorian Mode D to A is the pentachord, A to D is the tetrachord. The point where they overlap (in this case A) is called the Dominant (D.). If the overlapping point happens to be B, as in the Phrygian Mode, it is for technical reasons raised to C.

The Plagal Modes have the same finals as the Authentic Modes bearing the same name. They begin a fourth lower than the Authentic forms, hence the term Hypo, or Under, and their dominants are a third below those of the Authentic forms, except where this produced a B, as in the Hypo-Mixolydian Mode; in this case, the dominant is raised to C.

The following examples will show the difference between Authentic and Plagal Modes:

The last bass note of a modal composition will give the final of the mode.

The key signature of one flat is a sign that the mode has been transposed, and the final is in this case a fourth below the last bass note.

[1] Modes xi and xii with a Final B are not used.

Thus the following is Dorian transposed :

In modern editing of modal music any suitable pitch is used, and the series of sounds corresponding with this transposed form must be found.   For example :

Dorian transposed.

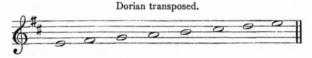

According to the principles of Musica Ficta, accidentals are employed in modal writing under the following conditions :

(*a*) When the Canto Fermo proceeds down one step to the final *at the end*, these two notes are accompanied (in two parts) by two proceeding one step up to the final, forming a major sixth followed by the octave, or inverted, a minor third followed by the unison.   The added part will therefore require accidentals as below :

MODAL CADENCES IN TWO PARTS

Authentic and Plagal.

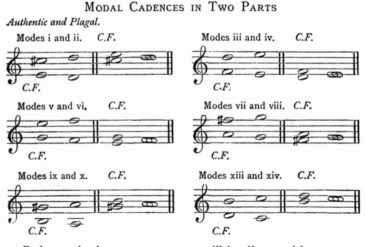

Cadences in three or more parts will be discussed later.

(*b*) The interval of the augmented fourth (F to B) or diminished fifth in melody, or as the extremities of a melodic passage,
is avoided by altering the second of the two sounds:

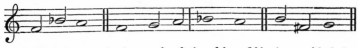

(*c*) The harmonic interval of the false fifth is avoided by
flattening the B:

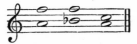

(*d*) The false relation of the tritone caused by the use of
consecutive major thirds in similar motion and by step is avoided
by flattening the B:

(*e*) A B lying between two A's should be flattened:

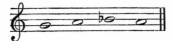

These procedures will serve for the present purpose.

CHAPTER II

COUNTERPOINT IN TWO PARTS

FIRST SPECIES

THE first way of adding a part to a C.F. is to write it in notes of the same time value, so that the two parts move simultaneously. The C.F. may be either the higher or the lower part. Formerly it was always in the bass, later it was put in the tenor, and eventually it found its way to the top; but there is now no restriction as to its position.

As Strict Counterpoint is concerned with the art of vocal part writing, certain limitations in reference to melodic progression are obviously essential.

1. The governing principle of melody, in all Species, is that of conjunct movement, judiciously varied by the use of disjunct intervals. An excessive use of either is inartistic.

2. A part should not proceed by any augmented or diminished interval. In the work of the English School we may meet with the leap of a diminished fifth or fourth, if the melody return immediately to some note within such interval:

But the use of such intervals is contrary to the practice of Palestrina.

3. A part should not proceed by the interval of a seventh, nor by any compound interval, either directly or with one note between—

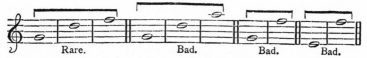

Rare.   Bad.   Bad.   Bad.

The following passage from the *Kyrie* of Palestrina's Mass, *Iste Confessor*, is worthy of consideration :—

Here in the bass we have the leap of a minor seventh, with one note between : but the phrasing makes it entirely unobjectionable—

Again, in his *Stabat Mater*, Palestrina writes :—

If such a melodic progression be used, care should be taken that the leap of the minor seventh is followed by some note within the interval. The following is unjustifiable :—

Fux.

4. The leap of an octave should be preceded and followed by notes within that interval.

All bad.

The following is interesting as being analogous to the previous example quoted from the *Iste Confessor*:—

Kyrie, Iste Confessor.

lei - son, Ky - - - ri - e.

The example quoted below is a rare exception—

PALESTRINA. *Magnificat, Tone vii.*

et ex - al - ta - vit.

5. The leap of a major sixth should be avoided, it was difficult to sing in tune.

6. The leap of a third followed by that of a sixth (or vice versa) is inelegant—

Professor Wooldridge's remarks on the principles of melodic progression in reference to Palestrina's technique may be quoted *in extenso*: 'The governing principle, technically speaking, of Palestrina's melody is of course that of conjunct movement;

this, however, is beautifully varied by the constantly changing value of the notes, and also by occasional disjunct intervals, which are permitted upon the condition of not continuing in the direction of the leap, but immediately returning by gradual motion towards the point of departure.

'This rule may also, of course, be deduced from the methods of Palestrina's predecessors since 1450, but there is in his application of it a certain final elegance, representing the ideal in such matters, which had been aimed at generally hitherto, but was now for the first time attained.

'Yet though Palestrina's method finally settles the questions respecting conjunct movement, and the general beauty and expressive qualities of the contrapuntal melody, exceptions to his rules may be found even in his own work, and especially as regards the continuance of the melody in the direction of a leap, a movement which sometimes, and most frequently in the bass or lowest part, is so to speak thrust upon him, from its occurrence in the given subject or from some other necessity.   Palestrina's conduct in such circumstances is often interesting, and remarkably so in the *Kyrie* of the Mass *Aeterna Christi Munera*, where the leap first occurs in the tenor or subject : here he seems, by frequent allusion, forcibly to draw our attention to the unusual figure, also showing (at A) how it might have been brought within the rule, and afterwards accepting it and (at B) repeating it again and again, in the bass, until we are quite reconciled to it.'   (*Oxford History of Music*, vol. ii, p. 376.)

7. More than two leaps in the same direction are inelegant.

8. Melodic monotony, whether arising from repetition of formula, or want of variety of range, should be carefully avoided—

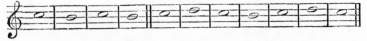

9. The repetition of a note in the bass (at the same pitch) is liable to cause a halting effect; the leap of an octave is of course entirely free from this objection—

Poor.   Good.

If, however, the repetition occurs between bars forming the end of one phrase and the beginning of another, there is no valid objection and in the application of the technique the point is of small importance.

The following are the principles of Harmonic Progression :—

1. It has been indicated that experiments led men to catalogue harmonic intervals as concordant and discordant in the following way : the octave (or unison) and fifth are termed Perfect Concords—

The major and minor third, and major and minor sixth are termed Imperfect Concords—

The second, fourth, seventh and their compounds are discords—

In two-part Counterpoint in the First Species only concords are allowed.

2. Consecutive octaves and fifths are forbidden, whether by similar or contrary motion—

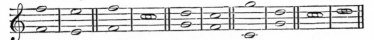

3. Except in the Cadence no perfect concord may be approached by similar motion; the objectionable effect is due to the exceptional prominence given to the perfect concord—

These are termed exposed fifths and octaves.

Exceptions to this rule will be dealt with as occasion demands.

4. The unison is only to be used in the first and last bars.

5. Of the three kinds of motion, similar, oblique, and contrary, the last is preferable, as tending to more independent movement.

Similar and contrary motion, however, should be judiciously alternated.

6. Not more than three consecutive thirds or sixths should be used, except when the parts cross, in which case the undue prevalence of parallel movement is avoided—

Bad.   Good.

7. If both parts move by step, the interval of the augmented

fourth should not exist between the C.F. and its Counterpoint
in successive bars—

This is called the False Relation of the Tritone.   If, however,
one of the parts, or both, move by leap no bad effect results—

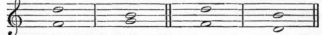

The mediaeval system of avoiding a False Relation was to
alter the second note forming the interval by the addition of
a flat, according to the principles of Musica Ficta—

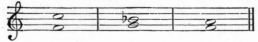

8. The parts should not overlap, but they may cross freely
in order to improve the melodic flow or to avoid objectionable
progression—

9. The first note of the Counterpoint must form a perfect
concord with the C.F.

In the last four cases, the C.F. begins on the dominant of the
Mode.   A modal C.F. may begin on practically any note.   When
the Counterpoint begins with a deferred imitative entry, its first
note need not form a perfect Concord with the C.F.

PALESTRINA, *Kyrie, Iste Confessor.*

10. Use imperfect in preference to perfect concords.

11. In approaching the Cadence avoid if possible anticipating the final of the lower part in the ante-penultimate bar—

Poor.   Better.

12. No note may be chromatically altered in the same part or in different parts in consecutive bars. This is found in the later English school.

13. The first aim in writing a Counterpoint to a C.F. is to get a good melodic line in the Counter-melody. The next step is to give the Counterpoint some relevancy. This can be obtained by employing the devices of imitation and sequence. As only note against note Counterpoint is employed the semibreve C.F. may be varied.

EXAMPLES

Mode viii.

Mode xiii.

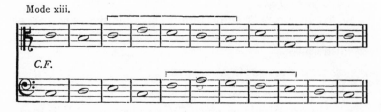

Mode vi.

Mode x.

Mode ix.

If the student be required to use the major and minor scales the following points should be noted :—

(*a*) The leading note must not be doubled.

(*b*) The leading note must not leap an octave.

(*c*) The minor scale must not be confused with the Aeolian Mode. The seventh degree of the minor scale is normally a semitone below the Tonic, and it should be so used, unless proceeding downwards to the sixth degree

A minor.

If the minor seventh is quitted by leap, a modulation to the relative major is implied.

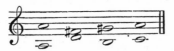

The major sixth of the scale may be used in proceeding to the major seventh :—

In other words, a part using the minor seventh or major sixth from the Tonic must be proceeding in the melodic form of the scale, which provides the justification for the departure from the harmonic form. Unless these limitations be kept the music will be confused in tonality. The Aeolian Mode only uses the sharpened seventh at the Cadence. In the minor key it is the normal sound, only varied for melodic purposes in descending. In ascending the normal minor sixth of the scale is varied. In both cases the variation is made to avoid the melodic interval of the augmented second. In A minor, F sharp is used to approach G sharp, and G natural to approach F natural.

(*d*) Diatonic modulation may be used in moderation, after establishing the tonic.

EXAMPLES

In practical terms

or it might have been grouped in triple time—

Example introducing modulation, and the use of the melodic minor scale—

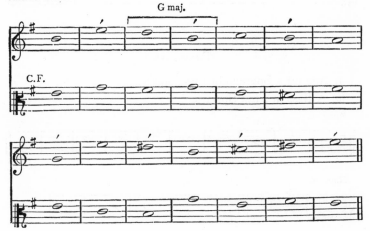

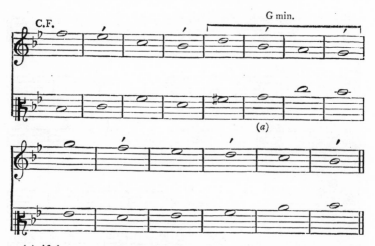

(*a*) if the parts cross, more than three thirds are allowable, as the prevalence of parallel movement, which is the cause of the rule, is avoided—

EXERCISES

1. Add (*a*) a Soprano in First Species.
(*b*) A Bass in First Species.

Mode vii.

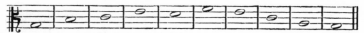

Mode ix.

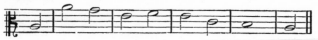

2. Add Soprano in First Species, using a deferred imitative entry.

Mode i.

3. Add Bass in First Species, using deferred imitative entry.

Mode iii.

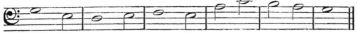

4. Add Soprano in First Species, using deferred imitative entry by inversion.

Mode viii.

5. Add (*a*) Soprano First Species.

(*b*) Bass First Species.

Major and Minor scales.

CHAPTER III

SECOND SPECIES IN TWO PARTS

Two Notes against One

1. It has been shown that the earliest attempts at Polyphony consisted of what we now know as First Species Counterpoint in two parts. It was also seen that one of the first means of variety was to make the parts move in notes of unequal value. Clearly, the simplest form of this variety was the writing of two notes to one. As it is the universal procedure in Polyphonic writing, that, except in the First Species, no two parts should commence at the same instant, the Counterpoint will begin on the second minim of the bar—

In the last bar, the Counterpoint has a note of the same duration as the C.F., obviously because the final of a Cadence must be on the strong accent. The Cadence then, is identical, as regards the sounds employed, with that in the First Species—

2. The first note of the Counterpoint must form a perfect concord with the C.F.—

(*a*) is an imperfect concord.

3. The first note of the Counterpoint in all the intermediate bars, that is between the first and last, must form with the C.F. a perfect or imperfect concord, preferably the latter.

4. The second minim of all intermediate bars may be :—

(*a*) Another concord—

if the second minim of the bar be another concord, and if it is approached conjunctly from the first concord, e.g. 5 to 6, 6 to 5, it may leap to another concord, provided the leap is taken in the opposite direction to the previous conjunct movement. For a leap in the same direction to an accented note is inelegant—

It may, of course, proceed conjunctly as at (*c*) and (*d*); in this case the second minim, though concordant with the C.F., is generally felt to be unessential.

Another concord taken by leap may proceed to a third concord by conjunct or disjunct movement, the selection depending upon the previous and succeeding movement. The best Second Species Counterpoint is that in which conjunct movement is judiciously varied by the use of occasional leaps. Generally speaking, the leap of the major sixth should be sparingly used, and only in oblique motion. The leap of a minor sixth may be used in moderation—

(*b*) A discord, which must be approached and quitted conjunctly—

In the following examples :—

a change of harmony has been made on the second minim. This is always allowable, though it may not always be expedient. The student must exercise his harmonic instinct in deciding when a change occurs, or is desirable or not.

Three illustrations from Palestrina are given :—

(*a*)   *Sicut cervus.*

(*b*)   *Kyrie, Aeterna Christi Munera.*

(*c*)   *Agnus Dei, Aeterna Christi Munera.*

The principle is perfectly clear. Notes concordant with the C.F. may be approached and quitted by step or leap, with no reservation except that of good taste. Notes discordant with the C.F. must not be struck with it, and must be approached and quitted by step. A few more examples (all taken from Palestrina's *Stabat Mater*) are added :—

5. Early theorists allow more than two leaps in the same direction—

ALBRECHTSBERGER.

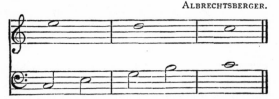

Such a progression is at best inelegant, and is contrary to general principle. If the C.F. were in the middle of a problem, the following would be better :—

and if at the end :—

6. It has been said that a discord may be used as a second minim in the bar, if approached and quitted conjunctly.

The theory that the second minim in the following example is to be considered unessential on account of the implied harmony of the first minim, cannot possibly find a place in Strict Counterpoint—

Therefore, consideration will only be given to true unessential notes, that is, those that are discordant with the C.F., the second, fourth, seventh, and their compounds.

Care must be taken to use these discords in a musical way. Under modal conditions no definite rules can be given, but the student should exercise his musical instinct, and not use unessential notes mechanically :—

7. Consecutive octaves and fifths are not advisable between the first minims of two consecutive bars ; they should never be used if the intervening minim is a discord—

It may be pointed out that older writers allowed consecutives if the first minim leapt an interval greater than a third—

and as a general principle an intermediate concord was held to save consecutives. But at present the student will have no need to make use of this procedure.

Consecutives should be avoided between the second minim of one bar, and the first of the next—

They are good between the second minim of each bar, if both notes in the Second Species are not the highest or lowest in the two bars—(see note, p. 45).

Bad.   Harmonic outline.

Good.   Harmonic outline.

The distance between the first minim of one bar and the second minim of the next is too great to give any effect of consecutives—

Good.

When either of the fifths is felt to be unessential no bad effect is produced if they are not direct.

Good.

Nor can consecutives occur between the first and third of three harmonies—

Good.

Exposed consecutives are forbidden under the same conditions as in First Species—

Bad.   Good.

8. The following does not cause a false relation of the tritone, as one of the notes forming it is felt to be unessential :—

9. The unison may be used in the first and last bars, and occasionally elsewhere as the second minim in the bar.

10. No note of the Counterpoint may be immediately repeated at the same pitch.

11. A note may not be chromatically altered in the same bar—

12. In this Species it is well to avoid the repetition of a melodic formula for more than two successive bars; a sequence having at least two bars as the limit of the formula is always good. In a more complicated exercise the student should use his own discretion.

13. The Cadences are as follows :—

Modes i & ii.

Modes iii & iv.

Modes v & vi.

14. As a precaution against later trouble, it is wise to discourage the use in the bass, on the first minim of the bar, a note which is the fifth above or fourth below the second minim.

The reverse procedure is much better, specially if the second minim be quitted by step.

15. As in First Species, imitation and sequence are desirable. Imitation of the C.F. at the start must obviously be by inversion and diminution :—

Mode i.

Mode xiv.

Mode viii.

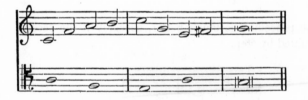

(a) A figure for Sequence should consist of at least four minims—

Mode vii.

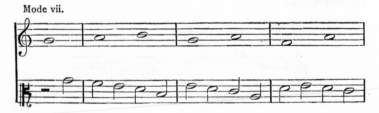

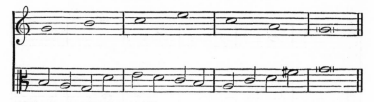

16. It is unwise to use nothing but a semibreve C.F. as it produces uniform rhythm, one of the things the writers of the period studiously avoided. In the following example the Counterpoint is in Second Species throughout :—

Mode i.

or the added part may now use First and Second Species indiscriminately :—

Mode x.

Mode iv.

Mode v.

Major and Minor Keys

1. As the minor seventh of the minor scale can only be used as a harmony note, if proceeding to the minor sixth as a harmony note—observe the following:—

Modulation to C major.   A minor.

2. The minor seventh and major sixth of the minor scale may be freely used as unessential notes, ascending or descending:—

3. Do not use the minor seventh or diminished fifth from the bass as a lower auxiliary note unless eventually resolving: the inversion is equally unsatisfactory.

poor.   poor.

good.

4. Do not use the leading note as an upper auxiliary note, over the second or fourth degree of the major scale :—

[Cf. rules of *Musica Ficta*]

5. The leading note should not be doubled either as the first or second minim of the bar.

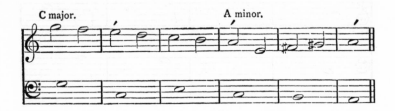

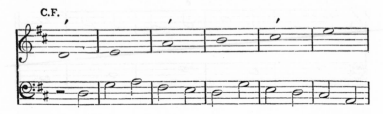

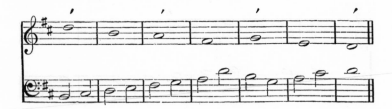

First Mus. Bac. Cantab., May, 1904.

Exercises

1. Add parts above the following in Second Species, Tenor, Alto, or Soprano, as expedient :—

Mode v.

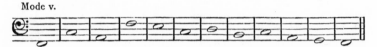

Mode vii.

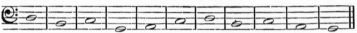

2. Add parts below the following in Second Species, Alto, Tenor, or Bass, as expedient :—

Mode i.

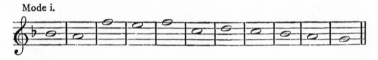

Mode iii.

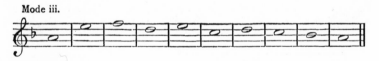

3. Add Second Species (minims or crotchets as the case demands) :—

Mode ix.

4. Modern Scales.

(a) Add Soprano in Second Species :—

(*b*) Add Bass in Second Species:—

5. Add First and Second Species as desired—begin in bar 2 :—

Mode ix.

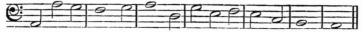

Consecutives. Though in actual sixteenth-century composition an intervening concord was held to save consecutives, it is advisable in technical work to bear in mind that uniform rhythm and pattern tend to make consecutives more prominent, specially in simple conditions, as here.

CHAPTER IV

THIRD SPECIES IN TWO PARTS

Four Notes against One

1. The Counterpoint begins on the second crotchet of the bar, and except in the first and last bars, four notes are written in the Counterpoint to one in the C.F.

2. The rules in First and Second Species as to the first note in the bar remain in force; in the Cadence the last two notes of the Counterpoint are the same as in the previous Species :—

3. If the second and third, or third and fourth crotchets are discordant with the C.F. the part must proceed in the same direction by step to the next concord. If the next step will not produce a concord, the passage must be rearranged :—

4. After using a scalic passage, it is inelegant to leap to an accented note in the same direction :—

5. *Changing Notes.*

Much ingenuity was exercised by the writers of the Polyphonic Period in the matter of the various uses of unessential notes. One particular idiom, known as the use of the Nota Cambiata, became quite characteristic. Dufay (fourteenth century) wrote thus :—

Mass, Se la face ay pale (Kyrie).

In (*a*) F is a passing note between G and E, leaping a third to the other side of E, and then proceeding to it by step upwards. This formula is seen in nearly all the works of the period ; particular mention may be made of Josquin's *Stabat Mater*, Palestrina's *Missa Papae Marcelli*, and Gibbons's *Hosanna*. A few examples may be of interest :—

(*a*)   Martinus Leopolita, *Mass, Paschalis (Kyrie).*

(b)

JOSQUIN DESPRÈS, *Mass, L'homme armé (Sanctus).*

(c)
PALESTRINA, *O admirabile commercium.*

(d)
PALESTRINA, *Benedictus, Missa Papae Marcelli.*

(e)

PALESTRINA, *Ego sum panis vivus.*

(f)

BYRD, *Mass* (*Credo*).

(g)   WILLAERT, *Motett. Ave Maria.*

(h)   GIBBONS, *Hosanna.*

In (*f*) and (*g*), through constant use, the real significance of the Nota Cambiata has been forgotten. An interesting seventeenth-century example is added—

SCHÜTZ, *S. John Passion.*

Consider the following cases :—

(*a*) In 1, 4, 5, and 8 the leap is from a discord to another discord.

(*b*) In 3 and 6 the leap is from a discord to a concord. And in all these the last crotchet forms a concord with the C.F. These are all examples of the true Nota Cambiata, for the principle in all is the same, e.g. the second crotchet is a discord, and leaps a third to the other side of the concord on to which it finally resolves.

(*c*) But in 2 and 7 the second and third crotchets are concordant with the C.F., while the last crotchet is discordant. It has been stated that these are also examples of the use of the Nota Cambiata, but in consideration of the examples that we have quoted from Palestrina in reference to the use of two harmonies in a bar in Second Species, and bearing in mind that the harmony may be changed on the second crotchet in

the Third Species, it seems probable that some such explana-
tion as the following
should be sought :—

E is concordant with the C.F., so is D, and so is B, that is,
the harmony has been changed on the second crotchet. Having
got so far, the composer would feel that he was using a familiar
idiom, and instinctively write the fourth crotchet as above, not
perforce of rule, but by habit of mind. For the true Nota
Cambiata requires the fourth crotchet to be concordant with the
C.F., and support to this is given by the following example
from Cherubini, who disallowed the use of the Nota Cambiata :—

The following examples from Palestrina and others will show
that in consequence of the frequency of the idiom, composers
lost sight of its original use. We may therefore say that if the
combination on the third or fourth crotchet is concordant,
the passage may stand.

(a) Original use.   PALESTRINA, *Kyrie, Missa Papae Marcelli.*

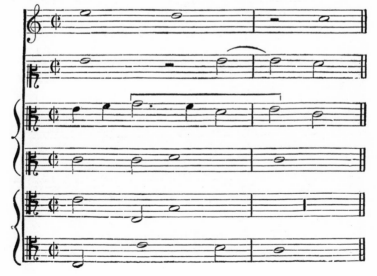

(*b*) As a Melodic idiom.   BUSNOIS (d. 1480), *Je suis venut.*

OKEGHEM, *Mass, Cuiusvis Toni.*

PALESTRINA, *Gloria, Missa Papae Marcelli.*

PALESTRINA, *Credo, Missa Brevis.*

It will be remembered that in Chapter III (4) it was stated that the following was inelegant:—

Now here we have three examples of it, A, B, C.   But this is due to the melodic curve of the original formula—

and in the majority of cases the phrasing is—

It is true that A and B are phrased—

A - - - - - - - - - men.

A - - - - - - - - men.

It will be seen that either the melodic curve of the original point or the phrasing makes these justifiable. For general cases the rule given in Chapter III (4) holds good. It is further to be remembered that the constant changes of harmony render the above quite satisfactory in effect: any attempts of this sort with a semibreve C.F. will be found to be harmonically crude, unless the C.F. leap an octave—

Good.

(c)   PALESTRINA, *Sanctus, Iste Confessor.*

Here we have the Third Species idiom, with the first crotchet tied: both the second and third crotchets may be considered as unessential, or it might be argued that the fourth minim produced a change of harmony.

(d)   PALESTRINA, *Ego sum panis.*

Here the idiom is divided between what corresponds in Scholastic Counterpoint to the second half of one bar and the first half of the next.

The above will serve to show some of the various uses of the Nota Cambiata. It has been said with great force that the device in its origin was 'the result of artistic feeling, and not of intellectual calculation.' Its various uses cannot always be defended by the rules of Discant, which are arbitrary; but they are always justifiable on aesthetic grounds.

Here we have the origin of what we term Changing Notes. Theorists mention the following variants of the original formula :—

These idioms are foreign to the period. In technical work the first may occasionally be employed at the Cadence. It should only be used there, and only as a last resource. It has evidently been introduced to avoid consecutives in three or more parts : but such consecutives were used in the period. (See next paragraph.)

The following is not a use of changing notes, but a change of harmony :—

6. *Consecutives.*

It has been pointed out that in the period an intervening concord was held to save consecutives—

PALESTRINA,
Credo, Iste Confessor.

Hence we find such procedures as :—

It must be borne in mind that in Third Species the semibreve represents two accents. To write several consecutive bars as above would not be good, for the parts would cease to be melodically independent. The student is recommended to avoid consecutives on successive strong accents unless a change of harmony has intervened—

Good.   Also good.

and in general to avoid them between the first, second, third, or fourth crotchet of one bar and the first of the next. This will enable him to keep well within the practice of the period. There is no need to parade close consecutives when they can be avoided.

Some one will say, is not the following equally bad?

If it is remembered that the time is $\frac{2}{2}$, the accentuation removes the effect. In any case, the notes are off the accent, but one would probably hesitate to write two consecutive bars with the same figure.

No such stringency as is enforced in text-books as to consecutives ever existed. Reliance must be placed more on musical judgement, influenced by the conditions of the period, than on mechanical rule.

7. The harmony may be changed anywhere. But it will be well to change it on the second crotchet only in using the Nota Cambiata idiom :—

8. Do not use an *auxiliary* discord on the third crotchet. It is not a practice of the period, and its use will cause later complications :—

9. If it be remembered that no discord may be used as the first crotchet of the bar, and that all discords occurring in the other parts of the bar must be approached and quitted by step, the following examples will be understood :—

10. The leap of a sixth (major or minor) should be avoided in notes of such short time value as crotchets; Palestrina never used it.

11. The extremities of a melodic passage should not form the tritone—

(*a*) Flatten the B.

12. Avoid disjunct movement throughout a bar.

Bad.   Bad.   Good.   Good.

13. The unison is allowed under the same conditions as in
Second Species.

14. Try to avoid running into the unison : it is permissible in
a case of emergency to run through it—

Tolerated.

It should however be stated that running into the unison is
frequently seen in the music of the period.

15. In writing Third Species :

(*a*) Let the part undulate.

(*b*) Avoid a preponderance of disjunct or conjunct movement.

(*c*) Avoid a succession of auxiliary notes on the second
crotchet of the bar.

(*d*) Aim at variety of range, variety of curve, and some good
scalic passages. The part should rise to at least one
climax.

16. The Counterpoint may imitate the C.F. in double diminution directly or by inversion :—

Mode i.

Mode v.

17. A Sequence of at least two bars pattern is good :—

Mode i.

18. The following are the usual Cadences :—

Modes i & ii.

(a)

(*a*) Best used in this form as completion of scale. This can also be used in other Modes.

Modes iii & iv.

Modes v & vi.

Modes vii & viii.

Modes ix & x.

Modes xiii & xiv.

The student will very soon see that all the formulae cannot be used with every Mode. A complete list is not given. The last two notes never vary.

Mode iii.

Mode ix.

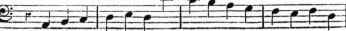

MAJOR AND MINOR KEYS.

1. The following is unsatisfactory harmonically :—

Key C.

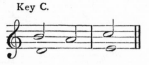

Hence :

2. Bear in mind the remarks as to unessential notes in the previous chapter, and do not use them mechanically. Remember that the minor seventh or diminished fifth from the bass requires resolution :—

3. The melodic form of the minor scale is freely used :—

Key C minor.

Two-bar rhythm.

(*a*) Nota Cambiata.

(*b*) The somewhat hard effect of the tritone E flat to A may be softened by the introduction of an accidental: though as A is unessential, the matter is of no importance.

EXERCISES.

(*a*) Add a Soprano in Third Species, beginning with an imitation of the C.F. in double diminution :—

Mode ii.

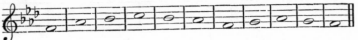

Mode ix.

(*b*) Add a Bass in the same way :—

Mode ix.

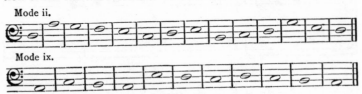

Mode xiii.

MODERN SCALES.

Add (*a*) Soprano in Third Species, (*b*) Bass in Third Species, introducing imitations and sequence :—

CHAPTER V

FOURTH SPECIES IN TWO PARTS

Syncopation

1. One of the most obvious ways of obtaining variety of effect, besides the use of passing notes, is to withhold the movement of one part while the other proceeds one step forward, and thereby comes to another implied harmony.

(*a*) If the part that is thus arrested in its motion produce dissonance on the first half of the bar, this is relieved by its moving one step downwards, and thus merging into consonance again—

Here we have examples of syncopated discords. The second minim of every bar must of course be concordant with the C.F. as it is the 'resolution' (*c*) of the 'discord' (*b*) which was 'prepared' at (*a*). The resolution (*c*) forms the preparation of a further discord (*d*). The combinations *ab*, *cd*, *ef* form what are termed 'suspensions'.

(*b*) If the first minim of the bar is concordant with the C.F. it is free to leap or move by step to another concord upwards or downwards, under certain restrictions stated below—

F 2

These are termed 'syncopated concords', and the time is
always $\frac{2}{2}$

2. It is true, as far as uncombined Counterpoint is concerned,
to say that Syncopation is a simple variant of First Species, in
that the accent in the Counterpoint is displaced—

but it does not always form a safe test as to faulty harmonic
progression—

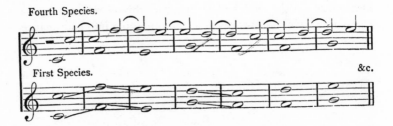

In accordance with the principles of the period, bars 1 and 2
might stand. The syncopated concord C serves to take away the
effect of octaves in some degree, specially when other parts are
added. Even bars 4 and 5 can stand. This is a common procedure in Palestrina. All these are syncopated concords, and
the fifths are not direct. E in bar 4 does not stand in place of
D, but is regarded as a separate concord.

The fact that moderns do not accept this view is not relevant.
The technique must be stated as it stands.

3. The Counterpoint begins on the second minim of the first
bar, and must form a perfect concord with the C.F.—

Good.　　　　Bad.

In the last bar, in all Species, the C.F. and its Counterpoint
consist of notes of equal value.

4. Let us now take the consonances, and experiment in the
formation of syncopated discords.

(A) Above the C.F.—

(1) though found in Palestrina and Fux, should be rarely
used.

(2) (4) and (5) form what we know as the suspensions—
$$4—3; \; 7—6; \; 9—8.$$

(3) is not, strictly speaking, a suspension at all; it is merely a
case of movement from concord to concord, 6 to 5, and is termed
a syncopated concord.

(B) Now experiment with syncopations below the C.F.—

(1) and (2) are what we term the suspensions 2—3; 4—5; (4) is
occasionally found—

LEOPOLITA. *Kyrie (Missa Paschalis).*

This is smoother than any other 7—8, for obvious harmonic reasons, e.g. from a modern point of view both E and D are essential. There is also an example in Tye's Mass, *Euge Bone* (*Agnus Dei*)—

But these are isolated examples, and quite exceptional.

(3) is subject to the same criticism as (3) above, that is, we have here a syncopated concord.

5. Palestrina generally uses the perfect fourth in syncopation. He does, however, use the augmented fourth—

Feria vi, *In Parasceve.*

But it should be sparingly used.

6. The 6—5 and 5—6 are syncopated concords, and the latter must not be confused with the modern retardation.

This is incorrect sixteenth-century technique.

To sum up, the note that prepares the discord (the second minim of the bar) must be concordant with the C.F., and the discord is resolved by moving one step downwards—

All bad.

7. It is better not to use the diminished fifth as a suspended discord, on account of the harsh effect.

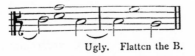

Ugly.   Flatten the B.

8. It has been pointed out that the second minim of the bar must always be concordant with the C.F.   The following are obviously incorrect :—

9. The False Relation of the Tritone may be found by reducing the score to First Species—

10. Two harmonies may of course be used in any bar.

11. Avoid melodic repetition—

12. The syncopation should not be broken, unless it involves melodic monotony or poor harmony; in these cases a single bar of the Second Species may be interpolated—

Melodic monotony   Good.

13. The unison is allowed on the second beat of the bar—

14. The last note but one of the Counterpoint must always be the note below the Final, as in the other species.

15. The Cadences are as follows:—

Modes i & ii.

Modes iii & iv.

Modes v & vi.

Modes vii & viii.

Modes ix & x.

Modes xiii & xiv.

If it is impossible to use syncopation in the Cadence, the Second Species may be employed.

EXAMPLES IN FOURTH SPECIES

First Mus. B. Cantab., May, 1904.

(a) Broken to avoid monotony.

The last two examples would be Modal if all the G's except in the Cadences were natural.

Mode iii.

Mode vii.

In using the modern scales the leading note may be doubled if syncopated.

Key C.

EXERCISES.
Modal.
(a) Add Treble in Fourth Species.

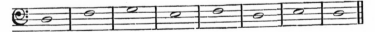

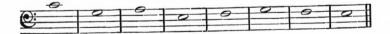

(*b*) Add Bass in Fourth Species.

Modern Scales.
(*c*) Add Treble in Fourth Species.

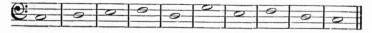

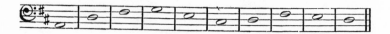

(*d*) Add Bass in Fourth Species.

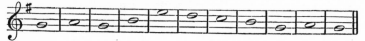

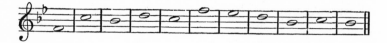

CHAPTER VI

FIFTH SPECIES IN TWO PARTS

Florid Counterpoint

1. Florid Counterpoint may be said to consist of the synthetical use of the technique of the four previous Species, together with a few variants of them, serving the purpose of more ornate texture, or improvement of melodic flow, and imparting to the whole artistic variety.

2. The following are the devices used to form variants of the four Species :—

(a) The combination of two Species—

This analysis is in reference to melodic movement, e.g.

Minims, Second Species.

Crotchets, Third Species.

Tied minims, Fourth Species.

Whenever a minim on the second half of the bar is preceded by notes shorter than itself, it must be tied into the next bar ; see (a) and (b) above. The only exception allowed is in the penultimate bar or at the end of a phrase. It is true that cases may be found in Palestrina's works where this principle is disregarded. But in the large majority of cases the procedure mentioned obtains, and therefore may be taken as a fixed idiom.

There is, however, one particular case that requires passing notice. In Palestrina's *Missa Papae Marcelli* the Nota Cambiata is extensively used, and the idiom constantly takes this form—

It may be asked, Why is any such rule necessary? The reason is that such a halt as—

would be purposeless, unless employed to introduce syncopation—

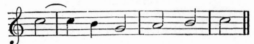

The case above, quoted from Palestrina, is of course justified by the nature of the melodic idiom.

(*b*) The use of ties other than those already explained, e.g. in which both notes tied are not minims—

Benedictus, Missa Papae Marcelli.

Nota Cambiata.

A tied semibreve should not be used in two-part writing, as the Counterpoint is thereby caused to lack interest.

The second of two tied notes must always be either of equal length with the first, or half the value of the first, and no note shorter than a minim should be tied into the next bar.

Both very rare : and never to be used except in six or more parts.

In (b) two crotchets are tied together ; such a procedure is so rare that it had better be discarded. It cannot be regarded as a variant of any Species, for the syncopation is introduced after its proper place. The second and third crotchets of the bar may never be tied, forming internal syncopation.

Morley in his *Plaine and Easie Introduction* (1597) gives the following as an order:—

but it has not survived; see *Kyrie, Aeterna Christi Munera* (Palestrina) for an example—

(c) The use of quavers.

Two quavers may be introduced in place of the second or fourth crotchets, and must be approached and quitted conjunctly. It is injudicious to introduce more than one group in any part in any bar, as the Counterpoint thereby loses dignity—

There are in Palestrina isolated examples of the use of four quavers in succession.   The rarity of such a procedure justifies its exclusion from the regular technique of the period—

Gloria, Missa Papae Marcelli.

The following uses of quavers, involving melodic repetition, are bad :—

The following are good : —

A study of Palestrina will show that quavers should be used sparingly.

(*d*) By the use of dots.

Their use between any two notes of one bar in two parts is not practicable—

A dotted minim, in only two parts, causes a halt on the second accent of the bar.

Dotted crotchets, involving the use of a single quaver,

form no part of the technique of Palestrina.   The idiom is fairly common in the English School.

(*e*) By the use of ornamental forms of the Fourth Species.

The following are ornamental resolutions of syncopated discords taken from Palestrina's works :—

A.

Aeterna Christi Munera.

These are all examples of anticipation of resolution, and may be catalogued thus :—

B.   *Credo, Missa Brevis.*

At (*a*) the tenor leaps to a note consonant with the bass before resolving.   At (*b*) the alto leaps to a note dissonant with the bass before resolving.

These are really modifications of the use of the Nota Cambiata, and may be catalogued thus :—

The leap or conjunct movement to a note higher in pitch than the note of resolution, and the use of quavers higher in pitch than such note, though permissible, will be found to be extremely rare in practice—

Rare.

In every case the syncopated discord must be resolved on the third crotchet of the bar.

3. Each Species is of course governed by its own rules; as a general rule, a change of harmony should be made only on the second half of the bar, and rarely on the second or fourth crotchets.

4. The first bar of the Counterpoint may begin in Second, Third, or Fourth Species. No part may begin with quavers, but two of these may replace the last crotchet in the Third Species—

(a) ⌐ ♩ | (b) ⌐ ♩ | (c) ♪ ♪ ♪ ♪ | (d) ♪ ♪ ♪ ♪ | .

5. No absolute law can be laid down as to the extent to which any rhythmic idiom should be continuously maintained, but the following recommendations may serve as a general guide :—

(a) Not more than eight crotchets should be used in succession.

(b) Not more than three untied minims should be used in succession.

In two-part work the Second Species should be sparingly employed; it is better to tie the second minim of any bar to the first note of the next.

(c) In two parts the First Species should only be used in the last bar.

(d) Aim at 'the greatest amount of variety consistent with true dignity of style' (Rockstro).

6. The cadences are the same as in the Second, Third, and Fourth Species, with or without ornamental resolutions—the limitations of the various modes will be easily discovered.

7. Avoid over-elaboration.

8. Avoid, if possible, allowing a part to return to the same point of repose in two successive phrases—

Poor.

9. One theorist remarks that a passing note may only be used on the third crotchet in unmixed Third Species. This is a good general rule.

But with the addition of another part forming a concord with the dissonance such a procedure is found—

PALESTRINA, *Aeterna Christi Munera.*

10. The ornamental resolution of a suspended discord must never cause consecutives between essential harmonies—

G 2

11. The important points to bear in mind when writing Fifth Species may be here summarized :—

(*a*) Do not use a passing note on the third crotchet, except in a part employing four crotchets in the bar. This is not often found, and in two parts the effect will be rough.

(*b*) Do not use an *auxiliary* discord on the third crotchet.

(*c*) Vary the points of repose, and in arranging these try to work towards a climax.

(*d*) Avoid a succession of bars with the second minim syncopated.

(*e*) As far as possible, mix the Species within the bar. A succession of bars of various Species unmixed is poor Florid Counterpoint.

(*f*) Movement should be fairly uniform. It is bad to have a few bars crowded with crotchets and quavers, followed by minims and semibreves.

12. Fifth Species is only one of the idioms used in actual composition, though it is in itself a combination of other Species. In the composition of the period the other Species are as common as the Fifth. And no part ever moves with the sustained animation of the technical fifth Species. The time is always $\frac{2}{2}$, never $\frac{4}{4}$ or $\frac{1}{1}$.

EXAMPLES

Mode i.

Mode iii.

Mode v.

EXAMPLES IN MAJOR AND MINOR SCALES

C.F.

(*a*) Not a suspension resolved on the second crotchet, but a change of harmony.

The same, according to strict harmonic principles :—

Either of these versions is correct Counterpoint ; the student will have no difficulty in seeing why the Macfarren school would condemn the former version at (*b*).

EXERCISES.

Any of the Canti Fermi in semibreves given in the previous chapters may be used for adding a part in Fifth Species.

CHAPTER VII

COUNTERPOINT IN TRIPLE TIME

SECOND SPECIES

1. IN a system of notation now obsolete, a semibreve might be considered equal to three minims : this value of the semibreve was termed the Greater Prolation, and was denoted by the use of a circle, thus :—

Its modern equivalent is of course $\frac{3}{2}$ with a dot added to the semibreve—

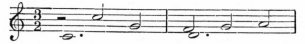

2. The Counterpoint begins on the second minim of the bar, and must form with the C.F. a perfect concord.

3. The first minim of each succeeding bar must be in concord with the C.F.

4. All discords must be approached and quitted conjunctly, except when the idiom of the Nota Cambiata is employed.

When the Counterpoint moves one step downward at the beginning of the bar, the leap of à third in the same direction, provided that the next note proceeds to the intermediate sound, is quite in accordance with contrapuntal practice—

5. A change of harmony in the bar is always allowable—

6. Two leaps in the same direction are unjustifiable—

All bad.

7. *Examples of Cadences.*

Mode xiii.

C.F.

C.F.

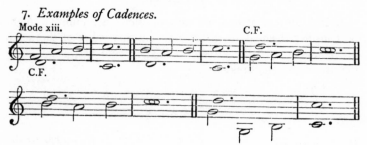

Mode ix.

C.F.

C.F.

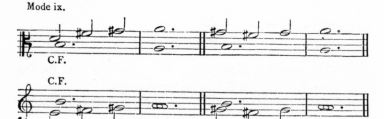

EXAMPLES

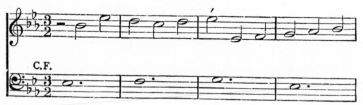

C.F.

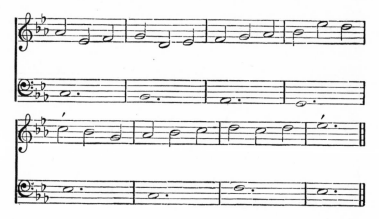

C.F.

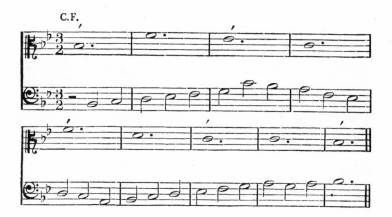

Mode vii.

THIRD SPECIES

No additional remarks are necessary.   The following examples
will serve to show the method of procedure :—

Key F. C F.

Fourth Species

1. The second note in each bar of the Counterpoint may be either a harmony note or a discord. The third note must be a harmony note, corresponding to the second in duple time.

2. A discord of suspension may be ornamentally resolved as in Florid Counterpoint, the actual resolution taking place on the third minim. It is equally good to resolve the discord on the second minim.

EXAMPLES

(*a*) Not consecutives, as the notes involved are mentally unessential.

(*b*) A possible ending.

FIFTH SPECIES

No further rules are necessary

Any of the Canti Fermi in semibreves given in previous chapters may be used. The semibreve will in each case have a dot added to it.

CHAPTER VIII

COUNTERPOINT IN THREE PARTS

1. In three-part Counterpoint the Consonances are as follows:

(*a*) Bass note with major or minor third and perfect fifth from it—

The upper parts may be arranged in any order, or at any distance expedient.

(*b*) Bass note with major third and major sixth from it.
Bass note with minor third and minor sixth from it.
Bass note with minor third and major sixth from it.

It will be observed that the perfect and augmented fourth and diminished fifth are Consonances between upper parts, all being consonant with the bass.

Consonances may, of course, be doubled:

2. The majority of the rules of two-part Counterpoint hold good for the extreme parts in all simple Counterpoint.

3. Make the harmony as full as possible on the first beat of the bar, that is to say, where possible employ three different sounds, unless it interferes with good melody.

4. The part-writing should be compact; the different voices should be nearly equidistant in the matter of interval; if a wide gap is necessary, it should occur between the two lowest parts. No two upper parts should as a rule be more than an octave apart. But the preservation of a good melodic line is the first consideration.

5. Except in the first and last bars, and occasionally in the use of Fourth Species, the unison should be avoided on the first beat of the bar.

6. CONSECUTIVES

(a) Exposed consecutives are usually disallowed between extreme parts, except at the cadence where the top part moves by step —

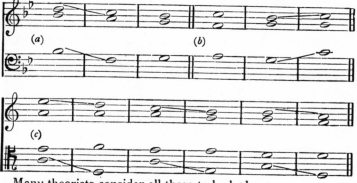

Many theorists consider all these to be bad.

(a) is found in Palestrina's *O admirabile commercium* —

H

(*b*) is found in the *Kyrie* of the *Missa Brevis,* and (*c*) is found in the *Stabat Mater*—

These are by no means isolated instances.   Observe also the following :—

Credo, Missa Brevis.   *Kyrie, Aet. Ch. Mun.*   *Credo, Ibid.*

It is clear that there was a good deal of latitude in such matters. The student must be guided by his musical sense.   He never need hesitate to write exposed consecutives between extreme parts if the top part proceed by step.

(*β*) Exposed consecutives are allowed between a mean and an extreme part, if the upper part move by step—

Good.   Good.   Poor.

The interpolation of a passing note does not justify exposed consecutives which would otherwise be condemned :—

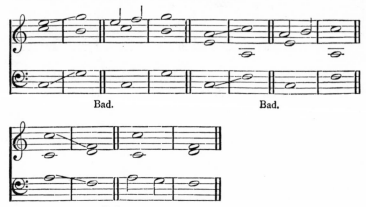

Bad.   Bad.

Bad.

If the unessential note be auxiliary, the effect is equally bad—

Bad.   Bad.

That is to say, the principle only applies when all the notes involved are essential.

(γ) One modern writer says that consecutive fifths are not allowed if one of them be diminished—

But there is no valid objection to them between two upper parts, if the lower part move a semitone.

(δ) Progression to the unison by similar motion should be avoided—

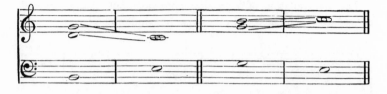

7. The parts may cross freely, but it is better that this procedure be restricted to upper parts as a rule. Much, however, depends upon circumstances.

CHAPTER IX

THE FIRST AND SECOND SPECIES IN ONE OF THREE PARTS

1. IT is one of the canons of elementary Harmony that if there be a note common to two consecutive chords, it should be kept in the same part; it is one of the canons of Counterpoint that, unless involving bad balance of parts or exposed consecutives, the movement of each part should be varied as much as possible—

2. In the Cadences, the C.F. always come down one step to the final, and one Counterpoint proceeds as in two parts. The third part must of course form consonances, and the last note in the bass must always be the final of the Mode. The final in the Cadence must be harmonized with the major third, or bare fifth; or all three parts may end on the final.

Mode i.

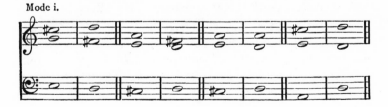

Mode iii.

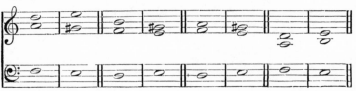

Mode v.

Mode vii.

Further examples are unnecessary.

Note (*a*) in Mode iii the bass of the Cadence must be F E or D E.

(*b*) in Mode v the B is flattened to avoid the tritone.

3. In writing three-part Counterpoint in the First Species, three different melodies may be combined, or the same melody may be imitated by the two Counterpoints using deferred entries, or an independent melody may be imitated. The imitation need only continue for three or four bars.

Exercises

1. *Modal.*

Add two parts in First Species.

(*a*) Soprano and Alto.

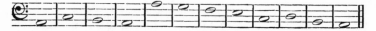

(*b*) Alto and Bass.

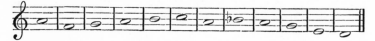

(*c*) Soprano and Bass.

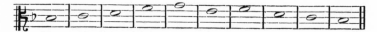

2. *Modern Scales.*

(*a*) Add Soprano and Alto in First Species, using deferred imitative entries :—

(*b*) Add Alto and Bass in First Species, using deferred imitative entries :—

(c) Add Soprano and Bass in First Species, using deferred imitative entries :—

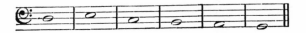

These Canti Fermi may be used for Exercises up to the end of Chapter XI.

Also the following :—

(Modal.)

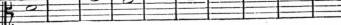

Second Species in one of Three Parts

1. The unison may be used on the second minim of the bar, if it secures a better melodic flow.

2. Examples of Cadences.

Mode xiii. C.F.

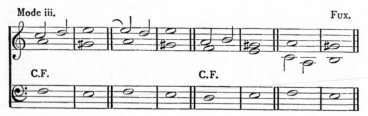

Mode v.

Fourth Species may be substituted for Second Species at the Cadence, if desired. But this procedure has probably arisen from the erroneous notion that certain consecutives should be avoided.

It is probable that the uniform rhythm of the technical exercises, which is foreign to the actual composition of the period, has led theorists to condemn consecutives which in their proper context would be much less obtrusive. An ear accustomed to regular rhythm is probably much more sensitive to the effect of consecutives on successive strong accents than one accustomed to sixteenth-century methods.

3. No two notes next each other in alphabetical order may proceed to an octave by similar motion—

4. The first note of the Counterpoint must be a perfect concord—

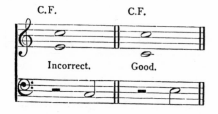

(a) the sequence justifies the tritone.

Mode iv.

Mode viii.

CHAPTER X

THE THIRD SPECIES IN ONE OF THREE PARTS

1. The cadences are generally as follows :

Mode i.

Mode iii.

Mode v.

&c.

C.F.

Key C minor.

Flatten all the B's except the last, and this will be in the Aeolian Mode.

In using the modern scales, the leading note may be doubled in Third Species, if it is in the middle of a scalic passage, or arpeggio.

Good. Good.

CHAPTER XI

THE FOURTH AND FIFTH SPECIES IN ONE OF THREE PARTS

1. As regards the accompaniment of the various syncopated discords the 9—8, besides being accompanied by the third, may be accompanied by the fifth or sixth also :—

Similarly, the 7—6 may be accompanied by the octave as well as by the third :—

and the 4—3 by the octave as well as the fifth, but not by the sixth :—

The last example is incorrect sixteenth-century technique. When the fourth is accompanied by the sixth, the latter proceeds to the fifth as the fourth descends to the third.   This occurs in combining First, Second, and Fourth Species.

2. As to the accompaniment of syncopated concords, the following examples will make things clear :—

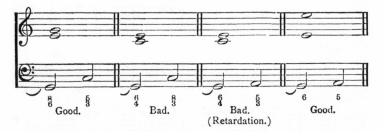

3. When the Fourth Species is in the bass, the upper parts may form a fourth, if the syncopated minim be a concord :—

In the latter case composers of the period would have written a fifth, A to E, or some other consonance.   The view is that when the bass is a syncopated discord, the next part above it is, for the time being, the real bass.   Moderns do not keep this restriction, and writers on strict Counterpoint have modified theory to allow of the second example.

4. Examples of cadences :—

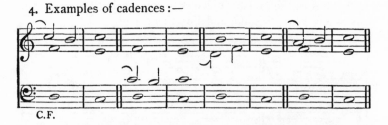

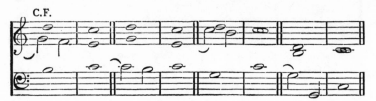

In using the modern scales the leading note may be doubled, if it is a syncopated concord.

PEDAL POINT

Sometimes the lowest part contains the same note for two or more bars : it then becomes a pedal point, and the next part above it is to be considered as the real bass.

PALESTRINA, *Aeterna Christi Munera.*
(c)

From a contrapuntal point of view the tenor is the real bass on the second minim, the bass again becoming essential on the third minim. A few examples are added :—

PALESTRINA, *Aeterna Christi Munera.*

CHERUBINI.

CHERUBINI.

Cherubini, while allowing that Palestrina uses the discord of the fourth without preparation in order that it may become its own preparation, makes the stipulation that the first discord be prepared by a concord, and the last discord be resolved by another concord.

Examples :—

Mode i.

Mode ii.

(*a*) It is hardly necessary to point out that some theorists wrongly regard such a concord as unessential. The following is sufficient to refute any such argument :—

PALESTRINA.

THE FIFTH SPECIES IN ONE OF THREE PARTS

Too frequent syncopation is unadvisable. The rules with regard to rhythmic and melodic variety already given in two parts must be most carefully followed. No further rules are needed in addition to those in the introductory chapter on three-part Counterpoint. The occasional use of an untied minim on the second half of the bar in uncombined Counterpoint is effective if it has been preceded by another minim.

EXAMPLES

The following Cadence is characteristic in the English School. (Nota Cambiata.)

CHAPTER XII

COMBINED COUNTERPOINT IN THREE PARTS

WHEN more than one of the added parts are in some species
other than the first, we have what is termed Combined Counterpoint.

THE COMBINATION OF SECOND AND THIRD SPECIES

1. Each part enters after a rest of the time value of the notes
of its Species. It is of course obvious that all three notes
struck on the first beat of the bar must be concordant.

2. The chief difficulties of the combination lie in the maintenance of clear, good harmony, and the conjunct motion of the
Second Species. The following are the methods of securing
this :—

(a) If the second minim of the bar be taken by leap, it is often
possible to make the movement to the first minim of the next
bar conjunct :—

(b) If the second minim be a true passing note, it, together
with all other moving and stationary parts, must form a good

harmonic progression on the third or fourth crotchet to the next bar :—

The use of a discord for the second minim in Combined Counterpoint will be exceedingly rare. If a discord in the Second Species form a discord with a harmony note (concordance) in the Third Species (on the third or fourth crotchet), that concordance cannot be approached or quitted by leap.

Incorrect technique.

Correct technique.

Students are warned to be very cautious in the use of discords as second minims in Combined Counterpoint. Such a procedure as the following forms bad music :—

It does not violate any stated principle, and is occasionally found. Probably our harmonic ears are more sensitive in this respect than those of men who thought horizontally. But in any case the procedure is not found very often: in fact it is exceptional.

(*c*) A change of harmony may be used :—

The Law of the Lowest Moving Part

3. What harmonic intervals are allowable in the case of the second minim and third crotchet? The general principle is that all notes struck together should be in concord, unless they are taken by contrary and conjunct movement :—

There are three exceptions to this law :—

(*a*) The fourth is allowed between any two parts when both are concordant with the bass :—

(*b*) The fourth is allowed between any two parts if the crotchet be a passing note :—

Sanctus, Missa Brevis.

Sicut cervus.

These are only a few of the many examples to be found in the scores of Palestrina.

We find in his works a great many examples of the bare essential fourth :—

Aeterna Christi Munera.

The probable reason why the fourth is used in the above ways and not the second or seventh is that the inversion of the fourth is a fifth, and we should have the following anomaly :

Both are equally correct technique.

(*c*) The use of a discord in Third Species against the leap of an octave in Second Species :—

4. It is generally advisable to avoid using the second or fourth from the bass as the second minim of the bar. Students waste a great deal of time in attempting to do this, when it is impossible.

Bad.   Bad.

5. Often a change of harmony within the bar will improve a passage :—

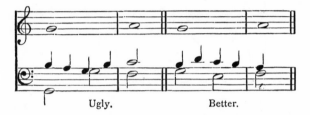

Ugly.   Better.

6. The consonance of the minor third and major sixth is often difficult to follow.   Observe :—

7. If the bass C.F. move down in thirds, it is an invitation to the Second Species to use 6 5 :—

8. Fourth Species may be used at the cadence instead of Second Species ; in this connexion note the following idioms :—

This is common in the English School.

9.   CONSECUTIVES

(*a*) Consecutives cannot occur between the first and third of three combinations :—

(*b*) Consecutives cannot occur with a change of harmony intervening :—

(*c*) Avoid the progression 9 to 8, 7 to 8 between any two parts.

EXAMPLES

Modal.

K

Modern Scales.

C.F.

C.F.

EXERCISES

1. Add an Alto in Third Species.

(a)

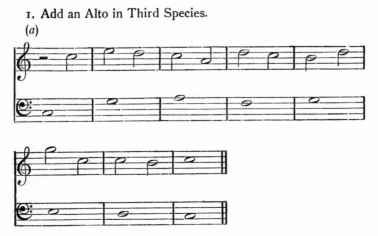

(b)

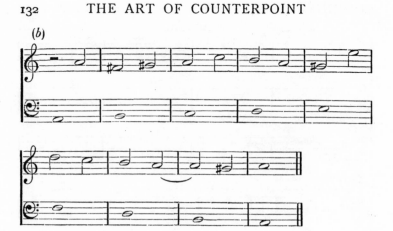

2. Add a Soprano in Third Species.

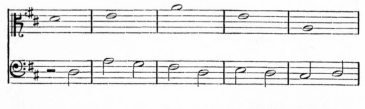

3. Add a Soprano in Second Species, Alto in Third Species.

4. Add a Soprano in Third Species, Bass in Second Species.

5. Add an Alto in Second Species, Bass in Third Species.

SECOND AND FOURTH SPECIES

1. It has been pointed out that no two parts should enter together, except several in the First Species. The Second Species therefore may enter on the first minim of the first bar, or either Species may enter on the second minim of the second bar.

2. As in the previous combination, one of the chief difficulties is the maintenance of conjunct movement in the Second Species. The following are examples of various ways in which this may be accomplished :

The last will be explained in the next paragraph.

The following examples are not recommended :—

3.   Prepared Discords

The scores of Palestrina exhibit a very useful variation of the original use of syncopated discords.

In this original use the accompanying parts remain stationary, while the discord resolves into concordance with them.

There are three variants of this procedure.

(*a*) in which the second minim of the Second Species moves to a different note of the same harmony—

(2) is liable to be very harsh and is not recommended, but (3) with the minor third is much smoother.

(*b*) in which the second minim of the Second Species produces a change of harmony—

Observe in (3) the origin of our chord of the dominant seventh.

Note that in all the above cases in (*a*) and (*b*) the first minims could have remained as semibreves while the discord resolved, and the resultant combination would in each case have been concordant, e.g.—

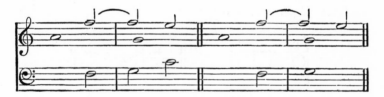

(*c*) In which the first minim of the Second Species, though concordant with the C.F., could not have remained stationary while the discord resolved. It usually proceeds by step into concordance—

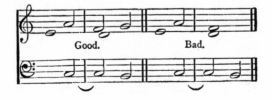

The following are examples of these prepared discords:—

Missa Brevis.

Note: (i) all the parts except the prepared discord form a concordance; (ii) when the discord resolves all the parts are concordant with the resolution; (iii) when the discord is in the bass the part next above it is the real bass.

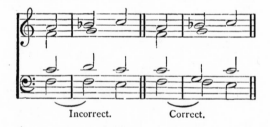

Incorrect.   Correct.

Distinguish between the following :—

(a) Good.   (b) Bad.

In the second case (*b*) the second minim in the bass (G) is discordant with the alto (F) and incorrectly approaches and quits
this discordance by leap.

4. The extreme parts may not approach a fifth, nor may any
two parts approach an octave, by similar motion, when one of
them is resolving a discord :—

Palestrina avoids this as follows :—

In combining the Second and Fifth Species, the following are
therefore good :—

The ninth should never be prepared by the octave :—

5. The fourth may be accompanied by the sixth, if the latter
proceed to the fifth as the fourth proceeds to the third—

EXAMPLES.

C.F.

C.F.

(a) · · · · · · · · ·

· · · · · ·

(*a*) There is no valid objection to this repetition of the formula. Note

is not to be criticized as

for no exposed fifth occurs.

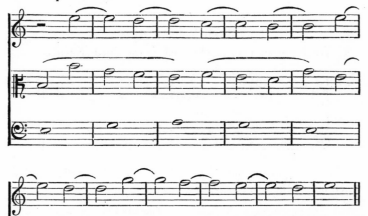

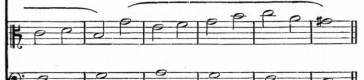

1. Add Soprano in Fourth Species, Bass in Second.

2. Add Soprano in Second Species, Bass in Fourth.

3. Add Soprano in Fourth Species, Tenor in Second.

Other Canti Fermi already given may be used.

THIRD AND FOURTH SPECIES

1. The harmony may be changed on the third crotchet—

2. No two parts should approach an octave by similar motion, when one of them is resolving a discord—

Poor.

3. Prepared discords may be used—

Note when the Third Species leaps, it is concordant with the C.F.—

By regarding the discord in its true contrapuntal light, the analysis becomes perfectly easy.

The last example is from Palestrina's *Aeterna Christi Munera*, and is a 7 6 treated in the manner of a prepared discord.

4.   CONSECUTIVES

As regards the criticism of Consecutives, examine the following:—

PALESTRINA, Credo, Missa Brevis.

Palestrina did not consider consecutive fifths objectionable between the first and third of three concords, if the first two were syncopated—

Agnus Dei, Missa Brevis.

nor if the first were a completion of a previous syncopation—

Credo, Missa Brevis.   *Ego sum panis.*

Even without these syncopations, that is, in ordinary Second Species, we find he had no hesitation in writing consecutives, if the intervening concord proceeded in contrary motion—

Credo, Iste Confessor.   *Confirma hoc Deus.*

He also wrote

Ego sum panis.

PALESTRINA, *Lauda Sion.*

These are not given with the intention that the student should be always imitating them. But he will see that the views of the period were decidedly liberal in such matters.

5. The suspension should not be sounded in the Third Species against its resolution—

Undesirable in three parts.   Good.

6. The following exceptional procedure in Palestrina's work should be noticed :—

Aeterna Christi Munera.

A minim preparing a discord should be a concord, but the group E, G, B flat is a discord. It probably stood because E flat would only cause further trouble. This idiom is not uncommon.

7. The principles explained on page 125 et seq. apply equally well here.

EXAMPLES

First Mus. B. Oxon., Nov., 1901.

C.F.

First Mus. B. Oxon., May, 1903.

C.F.

C.F. (Modal.)

L

For further Canti Fermi for Exercises, see the end of the chapter.

It is excellent practice to take a C.F. in Second Species, and add parts to it in Third and Fourth Species, thus—

C. F.

(a)

(*a*) the diminished fifth from the bass as a prepared discord is found in the English School.

SECOND AND FIFTH SPECIES.

1. In using this combination, the second minim of the Second Species should rarely be unessential. Avoid such procedures as :—

L. 2

cf. rules as to combination of First, Second, and Third Species, and criticize the quavers in the above as if they were crotchets, in regard to musical effect.

2. Constantly employ two harmonies in a bar, and prepared discords—

(a) Note dotted minims are now possible.

Third and Fifth Species.

1. In this combination the Fifth Species will be less active, on account of the constant movement in the Third Species.

2. This combination will entail some new technique—

(*a*) two parts moving in crotchets ;

(*b*) two quavers against a crotchet.

These procedures require detailed discussion.

Two Parts Moving in Crotchets.

1. The same unessential note may be taken by contrary and conjunct movement.

2. Parts may move in parallel thirds or sixths. Not more than three should be taken in succession.

3. An *unessential* third or sixth should generally be quitted in similar motion. But this is not by any means a law, or even a principle. Observe the following :—

Good.   Poor.   Better.

Criticism of these is based on harmonic instinct. But as no harmonic principles are involved, the student must rely upon his musical sense. He is advised in his earlier work to quit unessential thirds and sixths in similar motion.

4. On the second crotchet, two unessential notes may form a discord, if approached and quitted by contrary and conjunct movement. Such a discord should not be used in approaching new harmony, and care must be taken that it does not clash harshly with stationary consonances.

5. A discord off the accents may be struck against a consonance. Again this is better avoided between different harmonies.

Credo, Missa Brevis.

Some authorities say that in the above cases the C should be dotted

It is quite clear that there was no such restriction in the period.

6. A consonance may form a concordance with an unessential note

In using the consonance $\frac{5}{3}$, do not strike together at the end of the bar a consonance and the second or fourth from the bass.

Two Quavers against a Crotchet.

1. It was the practice of Palestrina that when two quavers were used against a crotchet, the first quaver should be concordant with this crotchet. A discord may occasionally be used by contrary and conjunct movement (English School).

2. There are two cases, and they require different technique :—

(*a*) The combination on the second crotchet. If the bass is stationary, it should be a good 'pedal'

Good

If the bass is moving in crotchets, the whole combination had better form a new consonance.

Good.   Bad.

(*b*) The combination on the fourth crotchet. Apply the same principle as that of the use of the second minim and crotchets in the combination of First, Second, and Third Species, except that the fourth should not be struck by leap.

Let one of the quavers be a consonance, and let the crotchet avoid the second or fourth from the bass. The following examples will illustrate this.

There is only one exception to this :—

Occasionally in the period we find the crotchet a true dissonance.
But the procedure requires discretion.   In any case the combination is sparingly used.

Fourth and Fifth Species.

The florid part need not be concordant with the C.F. on the
third crotchet, so long as the harmonic progression of all
the parts is good—

Double suspensions are possible, though rarely used in the period :—

Prepared discords may be accompanied in an ornamental fashion, thus :—

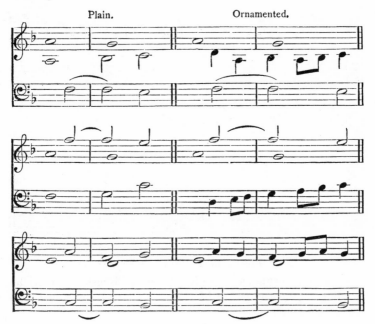

The use of dotted minims is of course freely allowed, if the third part strike a note on the third crotchet.

Fourth and Fifth Species in Triple Time.

Two Parts in Florid Counterpoint

1. All the technique has already been discussed under the headings of the various combinations. There are obviously two kinds of movement :—

(*a*) Simultaneous movement.   Two parts moving in minims, crotchets, or quavers.   The third is very rare : so is the first in three parts.   Two groups of quavers should move in thirds or sixths or take discords by contrary and conjunct movement.

(b) Oblique movement.

2. The Counterpoints should be equally interesting.   Neither should be too animated, or too quiet.   Use quavers sparingly.

3. Let the Counterpoints enter in imitation, using either the opening of the C.F. in some form of diminution, or an independent figure.

Modal.

Additional Canti Fermi.

Mode i.

Mode xiv.

The indication of strongly accented bars is for guidance in writing uncombined Counterpoint.

In the Major Mode.

M

In the Minor Mode.

4.
ALBRECHTSBERGER.

5.
CHERUBINI.

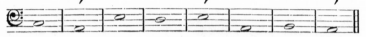

6.
CHERUBINI.

7.
CHERUBINI.

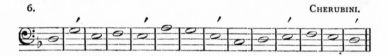

8.
FUX.

9

10.

CHAPTER XIII

COUNTERPOINT IN FOUR PARTS

1. THERE is practically no new technique to be acquired, so far as resource is concerned, in the Counterpoint of the sixteenth century. But as the number of parts increase, difficulties also increase. Therefore some licences become necessary. The writing in four parts, however, should be as strict as in three. One exception may be mentioned :—

In three parts it is well to avoid an exposed fifth or octave between an extreme and mean part unless the higher part move by step. In four parts this may be ignored :—

2. The working of uncombined Counterpoint in more than three parts, except where all parts are in the First Species, is an unprofitable study. It does not teach any useful technique, and generally resolves itself into a puzzle as to how to avoid consecutives. It was useful in three parts as teaching the use of complete consonances. As every complete consonance consists of at most three different sounds, the technique is covered. But for the sake of those who have to study this technique, a few examples are added :—

First Mus. B. Oxon., Nov., 1903.

First Mus. B. Oxon., Nov., 1901.

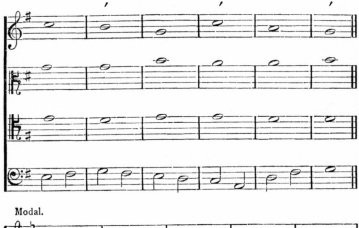

Modal.

C.F.

C.F.

Modal.

C.F.

The Beginning and Ending of Modal Phrases

1. It has been pointed out that there are some restrictions as to the notes upon which modal phrases may start. The Folk Music is very free in this respect, so that authorities differ in their statements upon the point. The following list is that given by Rockstro in Grove's Dictionary. The first phrase must begin on one of the Absolute initials :—

Mode I.   C (inverted seventh, note below Final) D. F. G. A.

„ II.   A. C. D. E. (rare) F.

„ III.   E. F. G. (rare) C.

„ IV.   C. D. E. F. G. (rare) A. (rare).

„ V.   F. A. C.

„ VI.   C. D. (rare) F.

„ VII.   G. A. (rare) B. C. D.

„ VIII.   C. (inverted seventh) D. F. G. A. C.

„ IX.   G. (inverted seventh) A. C. D. E.

„ X.   E. G. A. B. (rare) C.

„ XIII.   C. D. E. G.

„ XIV.   C. D. G. A.

Thus, the following in Mode III :—

2. Every other phrase can begin and end on one of these absolute initials. In addition any other phrase can begin and end on the notes called the Regular and Conceded Modulations.

(The ending of the *last* phrase is of course excepted, being on the Final.)

	Regular Modulations.	*Conceded Modulations.*
Mode I.	D. A. F. G.	C. (inverted seventh) E.
„ II.	D. F. E. A. A. (fifth above Final).	C. G.
„ III.	E. C. G. A. B.	D. (inverted seventh) F.
„ IV.	E. A. G. C. F.	D. B.
„ V.	F. C. A. G.	B. D. E.
„ VI.	F. A. D. C. (low).	B. (inverted seventh) G. B(♭).
„ VII.	G. D. C. A.	B. E.
„ VIII.	G. C. F. A. D.	B. D. (fifth above Final).
„ IX.	A. E. C. D. (low).	G. (inverted seventh) B.
„ X.	A. C. B. E. E. (fifth above Final).	G. D.
„ XIII.	C. G. E. D.	F. A. B.
„ XIV.	C. E. A. G. (low).	F. (inverted seventh) D. F.

The normal compass of the modes may be slightly extended. The mode is defined by the compass of the C.F. : the other parts will necessarily vary.

When the C.F. (or some part) comes down one step at the end of a phrase to one of these notes, the two notes are harmonized as a new Clausula Vera. In order to get the right colour into the harmony this Clausula Vera should be preceded as nearly as possible by harmonies that *contradict* it. Examine

Palestrina's Madrigal 'O che splendór' (quoted in full in my *Applied Strict Counterpoint*, p. 80) in this light. It is in the Dorian mode transposed. The following are some cadences :—

After the cadence the music works back into the mode again. In the English School it is common to find the final major consonance in such cases followed immediately by its minor form—

&c.

Of course in the actual composition of madrigals and so forth no single part is written first as a C.F.

The score would be written in the same way as it is done now. In the part-books there are no bar lines, for the rhythm is free. But the composer must have used bar-lines to keep things clear to his eye, not necessarily the regular ones of later music. Suppose a single line be given barless. How can we find out the accentuation?

Some few simple principles will be helpful :—

1. Notes that are felt to be suspended discords must be on strong accents.

2. Quavers must come on the second halves of accents.

3. Certain idioms always have the same accentuation :—

Examine the following :—

Second Mus.B. Oxford, Nov. 1920.

Fare - well,   dear   love, since thou   wilt needs be

gone   mine eyes   do   show   my   life . . . .

is   al   -   most done.

Two points are clear :—

(*a*) four quavers are so rare that it is safe to assume that each crotchet represents an accent ;

(*b*) the end supports this, the B flat is syncopated, the rhythm $\frac{2}{2}$ ♩ ♩ ♩ ♩ is very rare.

Three parts are added in Elizabethan style :—

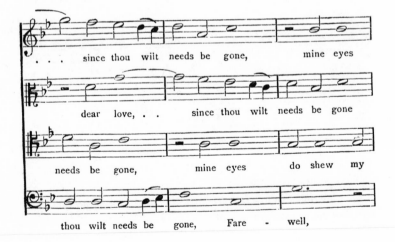

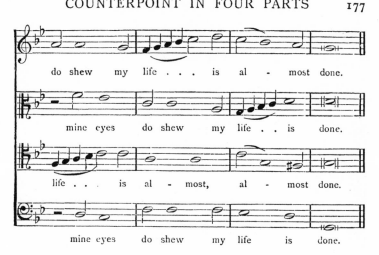

do shew my life . . . is al - most done.

mine eyes do shew my life . . is done.

life . . . is al - most, al - most done.

mine eyes do shew my life is done.

The question was set in five parts: a second alto may thus be added:—

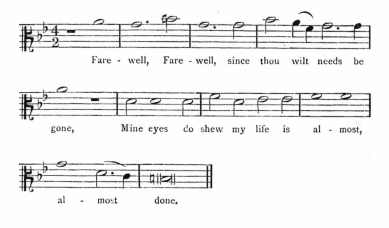

Fare - well, Fare - well, since thou wilt needs be

gone, Mine eyes do shew my life is al - most,

al - most done.

COMBINED COUNTERPOINT IN FOUR PARTS.

The combinations discussed in three parts may be repeated with the fourth part in First Species; thus there will be two parts in the First Species.

First, Second, and Third Species.

First Mus. B. Oxon., May, 1904.

First, Third, and Fourth Species.

First Mus. B. Oxon., Nov., 1900.

C.F.

First Mus. B. Oxon., May, 1904.

C F.

N 2

In four parts, we get a new combination in First, Second, Third, and Fourth Species. In connexion with this technique, note the following. When there are two parts in Second Species in the illustrations, one of them can be elaborated into Third Species:—

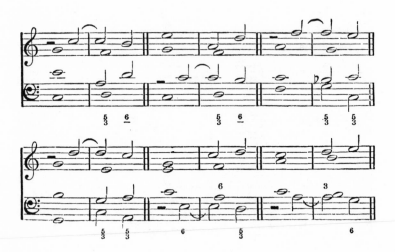

It will be observed that all the notes except the suspended
discord are concordant on the first minim of the bar; and that
all the parts are concordant on the second minim of the bar.
Ornamental forms are of course quite common.

The following example from Fux will be interesting, as
illustrating the views of the period in reference to consecutives.
The last part of the Second Species consists of six consecutive
leaps of thirds.   An emendation is suggested :—

Revision from (*a*).

Further examples :—

Third Mus. B. Oxon., May, 1905.

THREE PARTS IN FLORID COUNTERPOINT.

1. Distinguish between combinations which are felt as
   (*a*) passing notes, causing harmonic obscurity ;
   (*b*) passing concordances ;
often such possible combinations have to be discarded, and the
score simplified : sometimes the addition of another note makes
the effect satisfactory—

2. Just as, in three parts, the bare fourth was allowed as a
harmonic interval between two upper parts, so the following is
legitimate in four parts :—

PALESTRINA. *O admirabile commercium.*   BYRD. *Gradual. Beata Virgo.*

3. *Double Suspensions* may be used in Combined Counterpoint
in four parts, the additional part, by its florid movement, preventing any halting effect.

(*a*) Examples of double suspensions—

(*b*) With a florid part added—

Note also—

(*a*) Prepared discords and syncopated concords with Third Species—

(*b*) The same with Fifth Species.

(*c*) Ornamentation of Fourth Species.

5. All Florid Counterpoint should be imitative. Thus, the three Counterpoints may use an independent figure :—

Modal.

or two may use an independent figure, and the third imitate the
C.F. in some form of diminution.

First Mus. B. Oxon., Nov. 1904.

6. Watch for opportunities to introduce sequence :—

7. The Cadence may be extended, and some characteristic idiom introduced :—

8. In forming the score :—

(*a*) Sketch in the imitations first.

(*b*) If any part has been stagnant for two bars, fill it in first for the next few bars, and ensure its moving.

(*c*) Sing a part for the last few bars, as far as it has gone, and then try to let it move naturally from that point.

(*d*) Try to let each part have a climax, and vary the points of repose. Never hesitate to cross the parts for these purposes.

(*e*) Do not be in a hurry to get the parts in. They should not enter till they can do so in good imitation. This can generally be managed by the fourth bar.

There is an unfortunate tendency to overcrowd the Florid Score. Fluency is desirable, and stagnation is as bad as over-elaboration. The following is sufficiently florid in character :—

(*a*) the interval of the diminished fifth or augmented fourth between the prepared discord and a consonance does not seem to be used by Palestrina.   It occurs in the English School.

It should be quite easy now to write without a semibreve C.F. The use of words will necessitate the repetition of semibreves and minims.   The Species are used indiscriminately.

In these examples the rhythm is uniform. But one of the characteristics of polyphonic music of the sixteenth century is freedom of rhythm. This takes two forms :—

(*a*) duple and triple rhythms are often alternated in a part :—

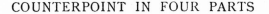

The glo - ri - ous com - pa - ny   of   the A - pos - tles   praise Thee.

(*b*) Different parts may be singing in different rhythms at the same time :—

BENET. 'Come, Shepherds, follow me.'

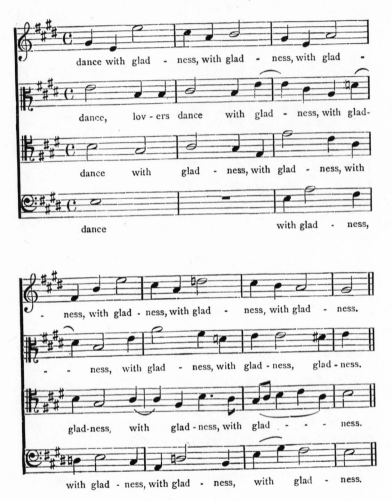

The student must not fall into the error of criticizing the accentuation of the above as being faulty. All this music was originally written without bar-lines. The rhythm of the Alto would be accurately interpreted thus:

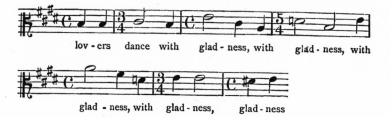

lov - ers   dance with   glad - ness, with   glad - ness, with

glad - ness, with   glad - ness,   glad - ness

The part-books have no bar lines, but in writing the score it
is thought the composer used bar lines about every eight minims
in duple time, and every six in triple time, for the purpose of
keeping the score clear to the eye. The student cannot get
very far wrong as regards technique if he remembers that
prepared discords *must* occur on strong accents, that quavers
occur on the second division of accents, and that harmonies do
not generally change more frequently than the accents.

CHAPTER XIV

COUNTERPOINT IN FIVE PARTS

1. HARDLY any relaxation of the rules previously given is necessary in five parts, and in any number of parts the strict idioms of Counterpoint should be observed. There is never any need to approach or to quit quavers by leap, or to use dotted crotchets. Dotted crotchets are found in the English School: but they are not used to get out of an imaginary difficulty. (See Byrd's 'Unto the hills mine eyes I lift', and 'Christ rising again'. *The English Madrigal School*, vol. xv. Stainer and Bell). Simplicity and clearness are the essentials of good style, and no single part must suffer from a lack of melodic variety.

Five parts in First Species.

Third Mus. B. Oxon., Nov., 1902.

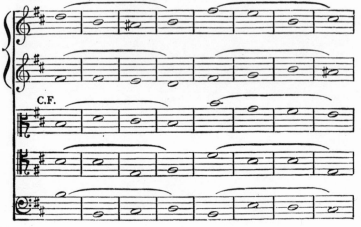

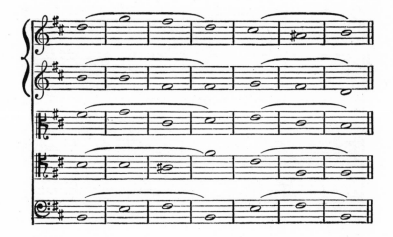

Third Mus. B. Oxon., May, 1904.

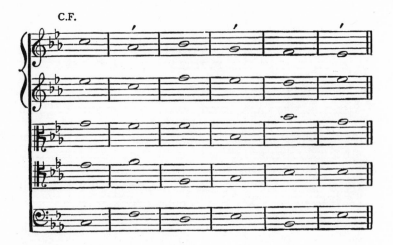

2. All the species combined:—

Third Mus.B. Oxon., Nov., 1905.

(*a*) First Species broken to obtain better effect.

(*b*) the diminished fifth is twice used.

The English School used many melodic intervals that are contrary to the Italian traditions.

FOUR OF THE PARTS IN FLORID COUNTERPOINT.

The parts may all enter in imitation of the same figure, or two contrasted figures may be taken :—

Third Mus. B. Oxon., Nov., 1903.

Or the start may be planned as follows :—

Aeolian Mode transposed.

St. Mary. (part)

CHAPTER XV

COUNTERPOINT IN SIX, SEVEN, AND EIGHT PARTS

1. IN six and more parts consecutive octaves and fifths by contrary motion may be used.

Palestrina used consecutive fifths by contrary motion, even in four parts—

Alma Redemptoris.

and the writers of the period considered them far less objectionable than consecutive octaves, which rarely occur in less than six parts.

Generally they should not be used between the same parts for more than two moves.

If using the modern scales the doubling of the leading note at the unison, which merely reinforces the sound, is open to no objection :—

2. The note preceding a rest should generally be a minim or semibreve, and a part should re-enter with some point of imitation.

A part should never rest for the purpose of avoiding a difficulty, but only to bring into prominence a 'point' or to afford artistic relief.

It is as bad to have too many rests as to have none. A phrase should be of reasonable length.

After a rest, no two parts should enter together. Neither should one part stop before another enters.

The phrases should always dovetail—

Unless careful attention be paid to this, a piece of six-part work becomes merely five-part Counterpoint, with one part distributed between two voices.

3. In cases of difficulty, the unison may be approached by similar motion. Also the rhythm ♩ ♩ ♩ | may be occasionally used with the minim untied. It is common in Palestrina.

4. The leap of a minor sixth may occasionally occur in crotchets.

5. In florid work, it is better that some of the parts should begin imitatively.

6. The simpler the style, the better the Counterpoint. There is no absolute rule that no two successive bars in any part should be in the same rhythm. The maintenance of one Species unvaried for more than two bars might be open to objection as florid work. But the First Species may be thus used in approaching the Cadence; and it may be used with discretion for two

consecutive bars in the course of a problem. The over-elaboration of the score leads to three disastrous evils :-

(*a*) confusion of harmony ;

(*b*) obscurity of harmony ;

(*c*) congestion of harmony.

7. Counterpoint in eight parts may be written for two Choirs of four parts each (S.A.T.B.). In the opening passages the Choirs should be treated in an antiphonal manner, but one should not stop before the other enters, that is, they should dovetail. When towards the close they sing together, the harmony given to each Choir should be as far as possible complete and satisfactory in itself. In such cases the basses of each Choir often move as follows :—

PALESTRINA, *Stabat Mater.*

The licences allowed in eight parts should only occur between voices in different Choirs.

The student is recommended to read Palestrina's *Stabat Mater* as an example of Counterpoint in eight parts for a double Choir.

As examples of ordinary six and eight-part work, the following may be studied :—Palestrina's Lectio III, *Sabbati Sancti* (Tom. XXXI), *Missa Papae Marcelli.*

Five-part work :—*O admirabile commercium.*

Four-part work :—*Aeterna Christi Munera* ; *Missa Brevis* ; *Iste Confessor.*

Also the following motets :—*Lauda Sion* ; *Ego sum panis* ; *Sicut cervus* ; *Sitivit anima.*

Mus. D. Oxon., 1903.

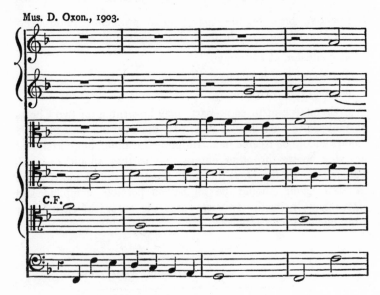

Six parts. All the Species combined—

Canon at the second.

Seven-part florid—

Mus. D. Oxon., 1901.

In this example some crotchets are discordant with the first quaver. It would be difficult to get an adequate flow of the parts without this licence.

Eight parts in the First Species—

Mus.D. Oxon., 1904.

Mus. D. Oxon., Nov., 1906.   'Introduce each part by some variation of the same figure.   All the parts should have entered by the sixth bar.'

Mus. D. Oxon., 1899. 'Commence the following in three parts, adding one part every two bars until they amount to eight, including the C.F. Begin with First Species, and introduce the others successively, combining them as you please, but ending with Fifth Species in all parts.'

C.F.

Mus. D. Oxon., 1899.

Q

CHAPTER XVI

THE ENGLISH SCHOOL OF THE SIXTEENTH CENTURY

It will have been seen that the technique of Palestrina almost results in an exact science, and for this reason it is invaluable as a standard authority. But no English book on Counterpoint can afford to neglect some reference to the great English School of the period, and having learnt the law and become proficient in keeping it, the student may now try to imitate the chief characteristics which differentiate the English from the Italian models. As this book deals only with technique, the student must refer to Dr. Fellowes's *English Madrigal Composers* (Oxford University Press) for a discussion of the inward differences between the two schools.

As far as the composition of madrigals is concerned the English School was late in the field. The period was from 1588 to 1627. The English writers had the advantage of studying the Italian models, as for example in the publication known as *Musica Transalpina*, and they were also bound to come under the influence of the new movement in 1600, which meant the birth of harmonic principles as well as the death of the ecclesiastical modes. Thus it will be found that the technique is largely experimental and progressive. The consideration of this music here will be limited to two main issues: (*a*) melodic idiom. (*b*) harmonic progressions.

Every student should possess at any rate some of the volumes of the English Madrigal School, edited by Dr. Fellowes, and published by Stainer and Bell.

For ecclesiastical music, Boyce's Cathedral Music should be consulted. If this is unavailable a large number of the works can be obtained in the editions of Novello, Curwen, the Church Music Society, and the Carnegie Trust.

In studying the scores, it is necessary to find out if the minim or the crotchet represents the accent. For example, in Byrd's *Songs of Sundry Natures* (1589), vol. xv (S. and B.), No. 8, Susanna Fair is given thus :—

&c.

And the following rhythms are seen :—

The unwary might be led to think that (*a*), (*b*), and (*c*) were new idioms, and that at (*d*) we had an example of a prepared discord occurring on a weak accent and resolving on its second half. It is true that (*c*) and (*d*) are found, but any one reading through the score will instinctively feel that so far as the application of technique is concerned, the time is $\frac{4}{4}$, and the opening bars in scholastic notation are :—

that is, each bar is equivalent to two bars of scholastic Counterpoint, and not one.

In this music we see the following melodic intervals: (*a*) chromatic semitones (Wilbye, 'Oft have I vowed', quoted on p. 215 of Fellowes, *English Madrigal Composers*; see also p. 193.)

(*b*) Augmented seconds.

(*c*) Diminished fourths and augmented fifths.

(*d*) Major and minor sevenths.

(*e*) Augmented octaves.

(*f*) Ninths.

The broad criticism is that while much of the music is in strict style, there are numerous cases in which the old rules are cast aside. Generally, some good reason can be found for the infractions, and it is to the credit of the English School that they broke new ground.

Further, the following is quite common $\frac{2}{2}$ ♩· ♪♩ |. It is never done to avoid the infraction of an imaginary rule, for example :—

BYRD.   *Right blest are they.*

It is said by some that a dotted crotchet followed by a quaver is allowed to avoid the unlawful percussion of a discord :—

Composers of the period never kept such a rule; in the example from Byrd the percussion of a *concord* is avoided by using the dotted crotchet! The following idiom is also found :—

BYRD.   *Unto the Hills.*

But the syncopated crotchet is more frequently used as a combination of triple rhythm against duple (e. g. really as a minim in triple time) :—

Ibid. (some parts omitted).

the complete first bass phrase is as follows : –

And   he   that   doth   thee . . . .   keep.

When we come to the question of harmonic resource, we see the spirit of enterprise and experiment marking a great deal of the music. It is impossible to formulate a theory from such a period, for it was transitional. It would be equally futile to attempt a theory of present-day harmony. The important thing is to try and realize why these things were done. Dr. Fellowes gives a list of innovations on the following pages of his book, which should be consulted :—pp. 109, 114, 115, 171, 172, 185, 196, 202, 220, 259, 261, 276, 297.

They comprise :—

(*a*) First inversion of the augmented triad, e. g. major third, and minor sixth from the bass used as a concordance.

(*b*) Chord of the augmented sixth used as a concordance.

(*c*) Chord of the diminished triad and seventh used as concordances.

(*d*) Simultaneous employment of major and minor third of chord. Minor third of chord with suspended fourth resolving on to major third.

(*e*) Unessential notes taken by skip.

(*f*) Unprepared six-four used as a concordance.

If the student were to use all these things indiscriminately, his work would cease to be even approximately 'strict'. It will be well to catalogue a few things that are fairly common, and not at the same time wildly experimental. It would be most unwise to try to use everything found in an experimental and transitional period.

(*a*) The diminished fifth as a prepared discord. Purists only used the perfect fifth :—

P. 4. *English Madrigal School.* Vol. xv.

(*b*) The seventh taken by leap in the Cadence :—

P. 6. *Ibid.*

(*c*) The unprepared fourth :—

P. 13. *Ibid.*

This seems to arise from the fact that it is the sixth exact repetition of the phrase, though it is difficult to see why it should not have been modified :—

(*d*) The unprepared diminished fifth :—

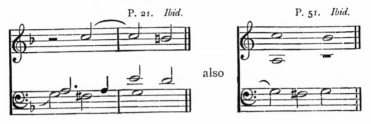

P. 21. *Ibid.*   P. 51. *Ibid.*

also

(*e*) The suspension 4 3 accompanied by the sixth and resolving before its usual time :—

P. 19. *Ibid.*

(*f*) The Nota Cambiata with the last note missing :—

P. 23. *Ibid.*

(*g*) Auxiliary note quitted by leap :—

P. 29. *Ibid.*

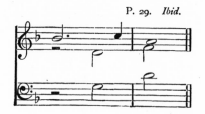

P. 31. *Ibid.*

(*h*) The suspension constantly resolves before its time in using the Nota Cambiata idiom :—

P. 42. *Ibid.*

(*i*) The following Cadential idioms :—

(1)

(2)

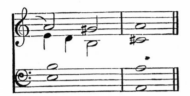

(3)

TALLIS.

Sufficient has been said to show the lines upon which the student may investigate the music for himself. The questions of notation, rhythm, and barring are all dealt with in Dr. Fellowes's *English Madrigal Composers*. In all the points discussed in this short chapter we see that the English were not content to be mere imitators. Both in melodic idiom and harmonic progression they showed initiative. They went far beyond the bounds of the original principles of musica ficta, and taken as a whole the music represents the transitional period between the Counterpoint of Palestrina and that of Bach. The secular music seems to show more innovations than the ecclesiastical work. It has been suggested that there is a need of a text-book dealing with English Counterpoint. It is quite true that the School 'shed upon our Elizabethan age a glory second only in lustre to that of its poets and dramatists.' Yet it would seem impossible to draw up any definite theories as to technique for a period which was so experimental in its methods, no matter how successful these experiments may be. Nor is such an attempt desirable: the student should certainly study this music and write some examples in the same style, but he must get his foundations in the Palestrinian technique.

PART II

MODERN OR FREE COUNTERPOINT

CHAPTER I

PRELIMINARIES

1. Before commencing modern Counterpoint, the following course should have been taken :—
   (a) Strict Counterpoint up to Three parts, including Combined Counterpoint.
   (b) Harmony up to the dominant seventh or ninth, including modulation, and the various modern uses of the unessential, diatonic and chromatic.

2. The grammar of Free Counterpoint is precisely the same as the grammar of harmony up to Brahms. No rules common to the two phases will be given. But the contrapuntal aspect will introduce some new features, which will be discussed as occasion arises.

3. One of the cardinal differences between sixteenth-century and modern Counterpoint is that the latter is based upon a preconceived harmonic structure. Harmonic basis must rule the nature of the parts, so far as sounds are concerned (see p. 5, Pt. 1). The student should always think of his chords first, and of the actual notes forming his score next.

4. Free Counterpoint deals with both vocal and instrumental style, sixteenth-century Counterpoint only with the former.

5. One of the chief faults to guard against in the Counter-

point of any period is over-harmonization, that is, the use of too
frequent changes of chord. The more elaborate the texture and
the quicker the tempo the fewer should be the chord changes.

6. The writing of Counterpoint does not consist in merely
adding notes of a shorter time value to a given part, though this
may form a technical exercise in keeping up a particular rhythm.
There must be some idea and development of idea in the
Counterpoint; it must not be merely a meandering set of notes.
Thus three chief methods of writing are deducible :—

(*a*) The Counterpoint will imitate the Canta Fermo in some
way :—

(*b*) The Counterpoint will develop an independent melodic idea.

(*c*) The Counterpoint will develop an independent rhythmic
pattern, which should have *some* sequential features to give it
point.

Points of this nature will be dealt with in detail as they arise.
But the student should realize at the outset that in elementary
harmony he is taught to write notes so as to form correct chords

and their decoration. In Counterpoint he learns to manipulate these notes so as to form good, logical, lines of tune. The fundamental principle of melody is the presentation of one or two ideas and their development, and not merely a succession of notes, however graceful their curve.

7. The modern major, minor, and harmonic chromatic scales form the basis of the harmony.

CHAPTER II

FIRST SPECIES

Note Against Note

1. In order to give the Counterpoint independence, or to bring into prominence imitation, occasional rests may be used.

2. All the parts should form definite phrases, not necessarily of the same length, or co-terminous, except at the end.

EXAMPLES.

(a) Counterpoint an independent melody :—

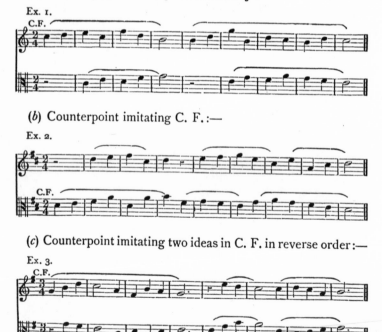

(b) Counterpoint imitating C. F. :—

(c) Counterpoint imitating two ideas in C. F. in reverse order :—

(*d*) Counterpoint beginning as a phrase in C. F. ends—

Ex. 4.

In the last example the note preceding the rests should be regarded as lasting in effect during those rests.

3. In modern work it is necessary to take note of implied harmony in two parts :—

Ex. 5.
C.F.

At (*a*) will be seen a weak use of the mediant chord.

At (*b*) there is a repeated note in the bass from a weak to a strong accent. This is only good if the repeated note be a prepared discord on the strong accent, or unless the previous strong accent has had the same note :—

Ex. 6.

4. *Harmonic intervals.*

What harmonic intervals besides those used in the sixteenth century may be employed?

Two Parts

(*a*) The seventh, and its inversion the second (or ninth), the diminished fifth and its inversion, the augmented fourth, of the chord of the dominant seventh.

As regards the seventh and second, they are better taken by contrary motion, except between two positions of the same chord :—

Ex. 7.

(*b*) Other diatonic sevenths or their inversions, if the part that has the seventh is proceeding downwards by step from the root :—

Ex. 8.

(*c*) The diminished seventh and its inversion :—

Ex. 9.

(*d*) The perfect fourth on the weak accent, as implying the passing six-four :—

Ex. 10.

THREE AND MORE PARTS

Any chord catalogued in a harmony text-book may be used. One salient difference between strict and free styles is that in the latter discords may be employed without preparation and thus they take the status of being essential :—

Ex. 10 a.

Strict.   Free.

Strict.   Free.

5. Be very particular about the use of implied six-fours.

(*a*) Do not use the $\frac{6}{4}$ on the strong accent, unless resolving into a $\frac{5}{3}$ on the same bass note or its equivalent :—

Ex. 11.

All good.

Poor.

(*b*) Do not use the $\frac{6}{4}$ as the first position of a chord except in the idiom given below :—

Ex. 12.

Bad.   Possible.

(*c*) Do not use the $\frac{6}{4}$ as the last chord upon a bass note unless the sixth and fourth could proceed onward by step to new harmony notes :—

Ex. 13.

$\frac{6}{4}$ 6   6
Poor.

6.   MELODIC MOVEMENT

(*a*) The greater the leap, the more necessary is it to approach and quit the leap inside the interval. In vocal work this should apply to leaps of the octave, seventh (minor only), and sixth. The leap of a major sixth may be freely used.

Ex. 14.

(*a*)   (*b*)   (*c*)

The leap of a minor seventh should have as its harmonic basis the same chord. The leap of a major seventh should be avoided as a rule :—

Ex. 15.

Bad.

(*b*) Avoid leaps of augmented intervals except in the course of a sequence. Leaps of diminished intervals are good if the next move be inside such intervals :—

Ex. 16.

7. Chromaticisms, involving sudden modulation in the middle of phrases, may be used with discretion :—

Ex. 17.

8. The Counterpoint may start with any appropriate harmonic interval, and the Cadences are freed from sixteenth-century conventions.

9. The rules as to consecutive and exposed octaves and fifths do not require re-statement. The following are good :—

Ex. 18.

10. It cannot be too strongly urged that a strong, sound, harmonic basis is a *sine qua non* of good contrapuntal effect. In two-part work it would be well for the student to figure his bass, showing the harmony he implies. And the parts should avoid all unnecessary ambiguity as to their harmonic implication.

11. This phase of technique may be studied at once in two, three, and four parts.

EXAMPLES

Exercises

1. Add Soprano in First Species, using a deferred imitative entry.

2. Add Bass, using deferred imitative entry.

3. Add Alto and Tenor, using deferred imitative entries.

4. Add Alto, Tenor, and Bass, using deferred imitative entries.

5. Add Violin part, introducing sequence.

6. Add part for Second Violin, introducing sequence.

7. Add Bass, developing an independent idea.

8. Add Soprano, developing an independent idea.

9. Add Counterpoint above or below, imitating (*a*) at (*b*) and (*b*) at (*a*).

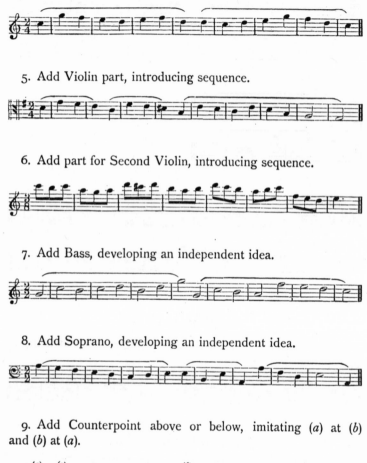

10. Add Counterpoint above or below, imitating (*a*) at (*b*) and (*b*) at (*a*).

(1) Let the figure enter here.

11. Add Alto, Tenor, and Bass, using deferred imitative entries.

CHAPTER III

SECOND SPECIES

Two and Three Notes to One

1. Employ all the modern unessential resource.

(*a*) Diatonic or chromatic passing notes (the latter in moderation), accented or unaccented :—

(*b*) Auxiliary notes, diatonic or chromatic, approached by step or leap :—

(*c*) Changing notes over one chord or two :—

2. The notes of the C.F. may represent one or two accents. When the former, one chord should *generally* be used for each note of the C.F.   When the latter, either one or two chords.

3. Beware of bad implied six-fours :—

 &c.

4. Consecutive discords should be avoided, except where all the notes concerned are part of the same fundamental discord :—

Poor.   Possible.

5. Laws as to consecutive octaves and fifths are more stringent than in the sixteenth century.

(a) Consecutive octaves and fifths must not occur between notes struck together on the accents.

(b) Consecutive octaves and fifths must not occur between the C.F. and the unaccented notes of the Counterpoint, unless one of the fifths or both be in effect unessential, or unless the harmonic outline does not show consecutives :—

(a)   (b)   (c)

Bad.   Good.   Bad.   Good.

Harmonic Equivalents.

6. Note particularly the treatment of the minor key as dis-tinguished from the Aeolian Mode :—

(a)   (b)   (c)

At (a) there is a modulation to F major.

At (b) the C.F. is correctly harmonized in D minor.

At (c) the original Second Species is correctly harmonized in D minor.

EXAMPLES

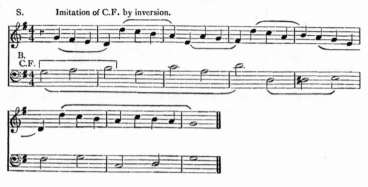

(a) A break may be made at a Cadence.

(a) A note may be repeated if occurring between the end of one phrase, and the beginning of another.

The following are merely rhythmic variations of the ordinary Second Species three notes to one.

&c.

EXAMPLES IN THREE PARTS

Two parts in First Species, one in the Second.

Exercises in Two Parts

1. Add Bass in Second Species.   Enter with an imitation of C.F. by inversion.

2. Add Soprano in Second Species.

3. Add Violin part in Second Species.

'CELLO.   (regard as B repeated
                                            in crotchets)

4. Add 'Cello in Second Species.

5. Add R.H. part for Piano in Second Species, three notes to one.

6. Add L.H. part for Piano in Second Species, three notes to one.

Exercises in Three and Four Parts

1. Add Violin in Second Species, Viola in First Species, the latter using a deferred imitative entry.

2. Add Violin in First Species, 'Cello in Second Species, the former to use Canonic imitation of C.F.

3. Add two parts in First Species below the following; pedals in Second Species (three notes to one).

ORGAN.

CHAPTER IV

THIRD SPECIES

Four and Six Notes to One

1. Examples of unessential resource applied to Third Species.

(*a*) Passing notes, accented and unaccented, diatonic and chromatic :—

Ex. 1.

&c.

(*b*) Appoggiaturas and auxiliary notes, diatonic and chromatic :—

Ex. 2.

(*c*) Various forms of changing notes :—

Ex. 3.

2. If the part be vocal the leap of a sixth in quick notes should be generally avoided. Such a procedure is, of course, perfectly good in instrumental style.

3. Consecutives.

(*a*) Consecutive octaves and fifths must not occur on consecutive first notes of the groups, whether the groups represent one accent or more :—

Ex. 4

(*b*) Consecutive octaves and fifths (both fifths being essential) must not occur at the same point or nearer in successive groups, if the reduction of the score to vertical harmony still reveals them :—

Ex. 5.

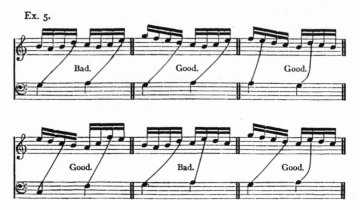

4. Such a device as the following is quite permissible in an exercise in which it is made a characteristic feature :—

Ex. 6.

But it would be out of place if introduced spasmodically. (Cf. Wagner's Overture to *Tannhäuser*, the end.)

5. In quick tempo, this species of Counterpoint should be instrumental rather than vocal. ' Rejoice greatly ' in Handel's *Messiah* is a vocal example.

6. Six notes to one may be employed in two groupings :—

Ex. 7.

7. The idiom mentioned in paragraph 4 may be used under similar conditions :—

Ex. 8.

8. Exercises in which two or more parts are in First Species (note against note) as Counterpoints to the Third Species are of little practical value. They are better if treated harmonically, e.g. as a filling up of the accompaniment. The parts need not then be independent, and consecutive octaves may occur between any parts in which the bass is not involved.

EXAMPLES.

The C.F. could be varied rhythmically thus :—

&c.

The above would be more practical thus :—

EXERCISES

1. Add a part for Violin in Third Species.

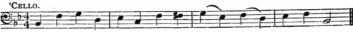

2. Add a part for L.H. in Third Species.

PIANO.

3. Add a part for Soprano in Third Species.

4. Add a part for Bass in Third Species.

5. Add a part for R.H. in Third Species (six notes to one).

PIANO.

6. Add a part for L.H. in Third Species (six notes to one).

CHAPTER V

FOURTH SPECIES

SYNCOPATION

1. IN the sixteenth century the suspension and its resolutic.
were generally notes of the value of accents. In modern work
there are no such restrictions :—

2. Further the preparation of the suspension may be a fundamental discord, or the syncopated note itself may be part of an
unprepared discord :—

And the suspension may resolve into any modern chord :—

3. Any parts of fundamental discords may be syncopated :—

4. Upward resolving discords may be used :—

5. From (c) has come the view that in any syncopation 5 6, and 6 5, the first note is unessential :

At (a) b is regarded as a retardation of c. Following this line of argument the fifths at (b) are good, but at (c) they are bad.

6. The suspension $^4_6$ $\underline{3}$ may be used :—

In two parts the suspension 5 4 may be used cadentially :—

7. When the bass employs the Fourth Species, syncopated concords should only be used between two different positions of the same chord, or between two chords moving from strong to weak, provided that a bad use of the six-four is not involved :—

8. When the suspension is in the bass, the upper parts form the factors of the chord without reference to the law of the lowest moving part :—

EXAMPLES

EXAMPLES IN THREE PARTS

EXERCISES

Pianoforte.

1. Add Bass in Fourth Species.

2. Add Treble in Fourth Species.

3. Add Bass in Fourth Species.

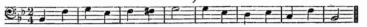

4. Add Treble in Fourth Species.

5. Add Treble in Fourth Species.

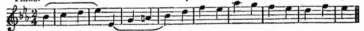

6. Add Bass in Fourth Species.

7. Add top part in Fourth Species, middle part in First Species.

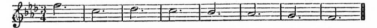

8. Add Bass in Fourth Species, middle part in First Species.

CHAPTER VI

FIFTH SPECIES

FLORID COUNTERPOINT

1. MODERN florid Counterpoint will naturally differ in its style according to the following various conditions :—

(*a*) Whether the style be vocal or instrumental.

(*b*) Whether the C.F. represent one or more accents.

(*c*) Whether the tempo be slow or fast.

2. VOCAL STYLE :—

It will be well to start with a free modification of sixteenth-century technique.

Beyond the points already mentioned, note (*a*) quavers (representing quarter notes) are freed from restrictions as to position and method of approaching and leaving. But care must be taken not to produce a jerky style :—

Possible, but not expedient.   Good.

(*b*) Half notes may be freely syncopated :—

(*c*) It is no longer necessary for the first of two tied notes to be of the same length or double the length of the second :—

Good.

(*d*) Such rhythms as (1) 𝅘𝅥 𝅗𝅥 𝅘𝅥., (2) 𝅘𝅥. ♪𝅗𝅥 𝅘𝅥 are good where appropriate.

But free vocal Counterpoint will differ from the strict style more in harmonic resource than in melodic idiom :—

This rather goes out of its way to be free : but it serves to show the difference.

Moderns use the crotchet as the normal accent, so that this would appear in $\frac{2}{4}$ time with notes in half the value of the above.

Such writing as the above demands a C.F. with notes representing at least two accents.

It is most necessary in deciding the style to realize whether the notes of the C.F. represent one or more accents.

If a C.F. be given in which each note represents an accent, it is best to regard it as a Second Species part, that is to say, the idioms of the florid part will be written according to the principles for an imaginary C.F. of notes twice the length of those given :—

It is quite unmusical to write over each minim here rhythms suitable for two accents :—

If the time signature were $\frac{4}{4}$, the above would be good.

EXAMPLES

3. INSTRUMENTAL STYLE.

The Counterpoint will differ from that in vocal work in that:

(*a*) It may be more elaborate in texture :—

In fact we may use over one accent what we used over two accents in vocal style (in diminution) :—

(*b*) Melodic skips, impossible or awkward for the voice, are good in instrumental style :—

There is no need to study this technique with any added parts in First Species.

4. In both styles a suspension may resolve after a rest :—

There is no need to tie suspensions.

EXAMPLES

Instrumental style.

EXERCISES

1. Add Soprano in Florid Counterpoint.

2. Add Bass in Florid Counterpoint.

3. Add (*a*) Soprano in Florid Counterpoint, (*b*) Bass in Florid Counterpoint. (No notes shorter than quavers.) Regard C.F. as Second Species.

4. Add part for Violin in Florid Counterpoint.

5. Add part for L.H. in Florid Counterpoint.

6. Add Bass in Florid Counterpoint.

7. Add Soprano in Florid Counterpoint.

CHAPTER VII

COMBINED COUNTERPOINT

First, Second, and Third Species

I. *Vocal Style.*

The Counterpoint will differ from that of the sixteenth century more in harmonic resource than in melodic idioms. Thus the following procedures are characteristic of free style :—

At (*a*) the six-four is treated as an essential harmony.

At (*b*) the harmony note B, though discordant with the minim F, is free to leap.

Again, any discords may occur between the second minim and the third crotchet :—

And the first minim may be unessential :—

Further, the following procedures are useful :—

It is hardly necessary to point out that in working in the free style, it is quite wrong to attempt to make everything characteristic of the free style. A fair proportion of the work may be quite strict, simply because it may be more natural or musical.

II. *Instrumental Style.*

In vocal work each note of the Second Species should be regarded as representing an accent, as a general principle. On the other hand, in instrumental style, with a quicker tempo, each note of the Second Species will be a half-note :—

The following procedures are useful in instrumental style :—

EXAMPLES

Vocal Style.
Moderato.

Instrumental Style.

T 2

III. *The Combination in Triple Time.*

(*a*) When the first two notes of the Second Species or the second note of the Second Species are essential, the treatment does not differ from that of duple time :—

Ex. 1.

(*b*) New conditions arise when the middle note of the Second Species is not a factor of the same chord as the first note.

If it is a true passing note it should only be used as in the examples given previously in this chapter; for example:—

Ex. 2.

If it is a factor of a new chord, it may be a chord returning to the original chord:—

Ex. 3.

or it may be a chord proceeding to another chord:—

Ex. 4.

This introduces an important point. Ex. 4 if carried to excess will give the effect of over-harmonization. Ex. 3 will not do so. The reason is that in Ex. 3 we decorate the chordal centre of C major, whereas in Ex. 4 three chordal centres are used in the bar.

All music reduced to its lowest terms consists of (*a*) chords, (*b*) their decoration.

This decoration is of three kinds, and each kind has its subdivision into (*a*) melodic, (*b*) harmonic.   This requires elucidation.

A chordal centre may be decorated in three ways :—

(1) By placing before it an unessential *note*, or chord resolving into it.   This is termed *Prefix* decoration, melodic and harmonic.

Harmonic decoration of this kind requires careful discretion. It is not always satisfactory, unless all the notes use this device—

or unless the decoration be prepared—

(2) By using between two statements of the centre melodic or harmonic decoration, termed *Internal* decoration :—

(3) By using between two different centres melodic or harmonic decorations forming a nearer link, termed *Suffix* decoration.

The particular case involved here is that of internal harmonic decoration.

The question arises, given a chordal centre, what chords may be used between two statements of it ?

A complete list is undesirable.   A few examples will illustrate the principle.

Take the triads on each degree of the scale.

MAJOR SCALE.

(*a*) Tonic may be decorated by dominant or subdominant :—

(*b*) Supertonic may be decorated by its dominant, cf. rule for lower auxiliary notes :—

Ex. 10.

(*c*) Mediant may be decorated by its dominant, or by the submediant :—

Ex. 11.

(*d*) Subdominant may be decorated by tonic or supertonic minor ninth :—

Ex. 12.

In decorating with tonic, avoid its minor seventh, and cf. rule for upper auxiliary notes.

(*e*) Dominant may be decorated by tonic.   Avoid dominant of the dominant, e. g. in C major, D major decorating G major.

Further diatonic decorations are common, also the tonic minor ninth :—

Ex. 13.

(*f*) Submediant may be decorated by its dominant, or by the supertonic :—

Ex. 14.

MINOR SCALE.

The series may be given in abbreviated form, and without comment :—

Ex. 15.

It will be observed that the scope of the minor key is limited. The abbreviated form given above seems to show how harmonic decoration evolves from melodic decoration.

EXAMPLES

1. Add Violin in Third Species and Viola in Second Species.

2. Add Viola in Third Species and 'Cello in Second Species.

3. Add Violin in Second Species and 'Cello in Third Species.

4. Add Alto in Third Species and Bass in Second Species.

5. Add Treble in Third Species and Alto in Second Species.

6. Add Alto in Second Species and Bass in Third Species.

7. Add Violin and 'Cello, combining Second and Third Species, alternate them between the two parts as you please.

8. Add Violin and Viola, combining Second and Third Species, alternate them between the two parts as you please.

9. Commence as follows, and continue forming a short Binary Movement, consistently combining First, Second, and Third Species (except at Cadences) in any order.

10. Add Violin in Second Species and Violin in Third Species in two ways, (*a*) using melodic decoration only, (*b*) employing where appropriate harmonic decoration. (C.F. employs chords in root position only.)

CHAPTER VIII

TWO PARTS IN SECOND OR THIRD SPECIES

1. PROBLEMS of this nature require a knowledge of the method of combining two unessential notes, or unessential notes with harmony notes when struck simultaneously, thus :—

2. The main difficulties have been discussed in Pt. I. It will be well to remind the student that on the point of moving to a new chord, it is injudicious to strike together a harmony note and the second or fourth of the root :—

3. If the perfect fourth be used, both notes should not be unessential :—

Bad.

The augmented fourth or diminished fifth should always be regarded as the third and seventh of a fundamental discord :—

Pedal.
Good.   Good.   Bad.

At (*a*) there is a confusion of the chord of C and the dominant seventh in the key of C.

4. Note the use of accented passing and auxiliary notes, as being characteristic of free style :—

5. Bear in mind the chief means of combination :—

(*a*) Parallel thirds and sixths.

(*b*) The same passing note in contrary motion.

(*c*) Root of chord + sixth.

(*d*) Root, third, or fifth + seventh.

There are more possibilities over fundamental discords than ordinary chords :—

EXAMPLES

EXERCISES

1. Add parts for two Violins in Second Species.

(a)

(b)

2. Add parts for Second Violin and 'Cello in Second Species.

(a)

(b)

3. Put 1 (a) and 1 (b) into Viola an octave higher and add parts for Violin and 'Cello in Third Species.

4. Put 2 (a) into Viola an octave lower, and add parts for Violin and 'Cello in Third Species.

5. To 2 (b) add parts for Viola and 'Cello in Third Species.

6. Add two parts in Second Species for Manuals (Organ).

CHAPTER IX

FIRST, SECOND, AND FOURTH SPECIES, AND TWO PARTS IN FOURTH SPECIES

1. THE chief new points in technique are :—
(*a*) A prepared discord may resolve into a new discord :

(*b*) A syncopated concord may also be followed by a discord:

(*c*) The Second Species may use an accented unessential note :

2. In vocal style, the Second Species should be fairly conjunct. But in instrumental style, where the Second Species is more rhythmic in character than melodic, and where leaps are not only appropriate, but easy of execution, the style may be as follows :—

TRIPLE TIME.

Vocal style.

Instrumental style.

Two Parts in Fourth Species

The following are the chief devices :—

(*a*) Double suspensions.

Ex. 1.

(*b*) Suspension and retardation.

Ex. 2.

(*c*) Suspension and syncopated concord.

Ex. 3.

Ex. 4.

EXERCISES

1. Add Treble in Fourth Species and Bass in Second Species.

2. Add Treble in Fourth Species and Bass in Second Species.

3. Add Treble in Second Species and Bass in Fourth Species.

4. Add Violin in Fourth Species and 'Cello in Second Species.

5. Add Second Violin in Second Species and 'Cello in Fourth Species.

6. Begin as follows, and continue in the same pattern for four or five bars :—

CHAPTER X

THE REMAINING COMBINATIONS

Now that the student is fairly conversant with free style, as opposed to sixteenth-century methods, it is unnecessary to point out further examples of expansion of principles. There is nothing new to be said about the remaining combinations. A few examples will suffice.

(a) First, Third, and Fourth Species in instrumental style.

Ex. 1.

The First Species could be varied thus :— &c.

(b) Two or more parts in Florid Counterpoint, vocal style.
Ex. 2.

(*c*) Florid Counterpoint in instrumental style.

Ground Bass, Third Mus. B. Oxon., May, 1905.

EXERCISES

1. Add two vocal florid parts.

2. Add two vocal florid parts, one above, one below the C.F.

3. Put (1) in Alto, an octave higher, and add three florid parts (vocal).

4. Put (2) in Bass, an octave lower, and add three florid parts (vocal).

5. Add two florid parts (vocal).

6. Add florid parts for Violin and Viola in various ways.

7. Add florid parts for Violin and 'Cello in various ways.

CHAPTER XI

COMBINED COUNTERPOINT WITH THE UNIFORM C.F. ELIMINATED

1. THIS Chapter deals with the various combinations already discussed, but with the uniform C.F. removed.

2. Below are two short examples, one of the combination of First, Second, and Third Species, one of Second and Third Species.

Ex. 1.

Ex. 2.

Some one will say, is not Example 2 merely First and
Second Species, and are you not drawing a distinction without
a difference? The difference is this, all true First Species notes
are essential. At (*a*), (*b*), and (*c*) the second crotchets are passing
notes. Thus the crotchets are written according to Second
Species principle, the quavers according to Third Species
principle.

It is a non-appreciation of this fact that makes students write
bad florid parts without the prop of the C.F.

The real point to remember is that chords should not as
a rule change more frequently than the accents, and that the
parts should be written according to a preconceived harmonic
basis. That is the real purpose of the uniform C.F.—to compel
this habit of thought.

3. Below are examples of two parts written on Second, and
two parts on Third Species principle; the harmonic basis being
given underneath.

Ex. 3.

Basis.

Ex. 4.
(Same basis.)

4. Second and Fourth Species principle.

Ex. 5.

Here again the top part is not First Species with tied notes. A primary condition of First Species is that the notes are essential.

5. Second, Third, and Fourth Species principle.

Ex. 6.

6. Two or more florid parts (vocal).

Ex. 7.

Ex. 8.

7. Third and Fifth Species.

Ex. 9.

8. Fourth and Fifth Species.

Ex. 10.

9 Two or more florid parts (instrumental).

Ex. 11.

Ex. 12.

First Mus. B. Oxon, 1903.

Third Mus. B. Oxon., May, 1905.

Moderato. C.F.

Third Mus. B., Oxon., Nov., 1905.

C.F.

X

Third Mus. B. Oxon., Nov., 1904.

Third Mus. B. Oxon., May, 1906.

Adagio. C.F.

X 2

The Adding of Florid Parts to a given inner Florid Part

In problems of this nature we are confronted by another difficulty, the formation of a melody. Many students are in the habit of working these problems on the same principles as those of Scholastic Counterpoint, forgetting that modern work demands modern principles, such as the systematic use of formula, the evolution of rhythmic phrases balancing one another, and so forth. In other words the C.F. is not a part that should be treated in the imitative manner of the Polyphonic Period, but as a component of a piece of modern texture.

Third Mus. B. Oxon., Nov., 1905.

Mus. D. Oxon., Nov., 1905.

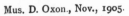

Third Mus. B. Oxon., Nov., 1904.

Mus. D. Oxon., 1897.
Andante.

Third Mus.B. Oxon., May, 1905.

Mus.D. Oxon., Nov. 1904.

SIMPLE EXERCISES

1. Add Bass in Florid Counterpoint.

2. Add Soprano in Florid Counterpoint.

3. Add 'Cello in Florid Counterpoint.

4. Add a florid part above the following :—

PIANO.

5. Add a florid part below the following :—

(a)

(b)

(*b*) the florid part must be less active than usual, owing to the continuous movement in the C.F.

6. Add Alto and Bass in Florid Counterpoint.

7. Add Second Violin and 'Cello in Florid Counterpoint.

8. Begin as follows and continue in Florid Style.

CHAPTER XII

VOCAL COUNTERPOINT OF VARIED CHARACTERS

1. CONTRAPUNTAL work in general assumes as a rule one of two forms in texture :—

(*a*) A part in long notes, to which we add parts moving in elaborate texture.

(*b*) A score in which all the parts are of the same florid character.

The former type is not confined to merely technical exercises. The Choral Preludes of Bach afford many examples. But the type is included under this heading because the long notes are not always of the same time value. Further, in such cases the C.F. ceases to be a mere prop, and is a real factor of the score, often supplying the formulae for the Counterpoints.

2. It will be well to consider one or two elementary cases.

(*a*) Add a Treble in free style to this tune in the Tenor :—

Ex. 1.

It should be fairly obvious that the Counterpoint must be in shorter notes than the C.F. Two procedures are possible, (*a*) to imitate the C.F. in some form of diminution, (*b*) to develop an independent figure.

Ex. 2.

(*b*) Add a Treble part in free style to this tune in the Tenor.

Ex. 3.

This C.F. is more active than that in the last example. It would therefore be appropriate to add a part in the same style.

Ex. 4.

it is true that the C.F. is not in reality much more active than the previous one (♩=♩) but it seems to require a quicker tempo.

3. Vocal Counterpoint on a Chorale, mostly in minims ($\frac{2}{2}$) :—

(a) If the tempo be fairly quick, the Counterpoints will not generally use notes shorter than crotchets. The lines of the Chorale will be separated by rests, and the parts will imitate each line in some form of diminution. It is generally better to start imitations of the next line before the previous line ends.

Ex. 5.

(*b*) If the tempo be quite slow, the following style would be appropriate :—

Ex. 6.

4. Vocal Counterpoint on a florid theme.

(*a*) Two parts.

This will generally assume one of three forms :—

(1) The Counterpoint will imitate the C.F.

(2) The C.F. will give out two ideas, *a, b*.

The Counterpoint will combine with the C.F. in the reverse order, *b, a*.

(3) The Counterpoint will develop an independent idea.

Find the time value of the accents, and generally avoid changing the harmony more frequently than the accents. The training with a C.F. in long notes should have taught the student to write his parts with a clear conception of the underlying harmony. Examples of each of the above, all in $\frac{2}{2}$ time :—

Ex. 7.

(*b*) Three or more parts.

In three or four parts, the entries will generally be in imitation of the C.F.

Ex. 8.

In four or more parts we can start with two contrasted formulae, and let the parts imitate the one or the other in any order that is expedient.

Ex. 10.

(c) In four parts if the C.F. give out two ideas, *a, b,* the following is a good plan :—

C.F.	S.	a	—	b	—
	A.	b	—	a	---
	T.	—	b	—	a
	B.	—	a	---	b

This cannot of course be rigidly followed, but the general principle can be applied.

Ex. 9.

5. Advanced students may like to see a problem in eight parts.

The vocal fugue, or work in fugato style, may be attempted when fugal form and Double Counterpoint have been studied.

EXERCISES

1. Treat the following C.F. in the ways undermentioned :—

(*a*) Add Soprano in imitative Counterpoint (two ways).
(*b*) Add Bass in imitative Counterpoint (two ways).
(*c*) Add Soprano and Bass in imitative Counterpoint (two ways). *See* par. 3 (*a*), (*b*), p. 321.

2. Treat the following C.F. in the ways undermentioned :—

(*a*) Add Soprano in imitative Counterpoint. *See* Ex. 4, p. 320.
(*b*) Add S. A. T. in imitative Counterpoint, making use of the two given figures. *See* par. 4 (*c*), p. 326.

3. Add Soprano in two ways. *See* par. 4 (*a*) (1), and (3), p. 323.

4. Add Bass in two ways. *See* par. 4 (*a*) (2), and (3), p. 323.

CHAPTER XIII

INSTRUMENTAL COUNTERPOINT OF VARIED CHARACTER

1. THIS technique may be applied in the following forms :—

(*a*) Two and three part Inventions. *See* Bach Inventions.

(*b*) Allemandes and Gigues. *See* the Bach and Handel Suites.

(*c*) Choral Preludes for the Organ.

(*d*) Instrumental Fugues, and Fantasies for Strings.

(*e*) Advanced Modulation problems.

2. This is not a book on applied technique, so that the form of the various types mentioned above must be studied by referring to well-known works.

But it may be said here that examples under headings (*a*) and (*b*) will be in Binary Form.

3. *Inventions*, &c.

BROAD PLAN

(*a*) Two halves, the first setting out from the Tonic, and ending in the complementary key, the second half setting out in this key and working back to the Tonic.

(*b*) The openings of each half correspond, and the endings sometimes do so.

For example, if the opening began with the following figure :—

Ex 1.

The beginning of the second half would start with this material in A major with the parts inverted, or with the figure treated by inversion.

Ex. 2.

If the first part ended with a modulation through B minor to A major, the second part could end with this material transposed a fifth lower or fourth higher, thus modulating through E minor back to D major.

Or we can start with two contrasted ideas which may, at the beginning of the second half, be presented in inverted forms, varied if necessary.

Ex. 3.

4. Allemandes and Gigues are written on the same general plan, though they may exhibit less device. The Gigue will of course be light in character and in some compound time. The Allemande is somewhat severe in style. In order to give the music point, frequent use should be made of sequence. But after one repetition the figure should be varied.

Point may also be obtained by working towards some definite climax in pitch, and then relaxing the tension.

A melodic line must not be aimless, it must be leading to some definite goal.

Choral Preludes

5. The style may be either simple or elaborate. Bach affords plenty of examples of both. The common types are :—

(*a*) The Chorale accompanied by Counterpoints framed on its various phrases in some form of diminution.

(*b*) The Chorale accompanied by independent figures.

(*c*) The Chorale itself elaborated and accompanied in either of the above ways.

Examples for Study

Bach.	Choral Preludes.	Peters.
Parry.	,, ,,	Novello.
Wood in C.	,, ,,	Stainer & Bell.
Max Reger.	,, ,,	Novello.
Brahms.	,, ,,	Simrock.
Harwood.	Communion on ' Irish '.	Novello.

The lines of the Chorale are usually marked off by rests. The Chorale may be written in any time appropriate to the style adopted. In some modern Choral Preludes the texture is harmonic rather than contrapuntal (*see* Brahms). For the present purpose, the latter style is required.

Examples

Method (*a*)	Bach.	Valet will ich dir geben.	(B flat.)
Method (*b*)	Bach.	Valet will ich dir geben.	(D major.)
	Bach.	Wachet auf.	
	Parry.	Rockingham.	
Method (*c*)	Harwood.	Communion on ' Irish '.	
	Bach.	Nun komm' der Heiden Heiland.	

6.   INSTRUMENTAL FUGUES

A study of fugal construction is necessary; but there is nothing new in technique except Double Counterpoint. Reference must be made to books on Fugue and Double Counterpoint.

7.   FANTASIES FOR STRINGS

A String Fantasy or Fancy was originally (at the end of the sixteenth century) the instrumental counterpart of the vocal madrigal, and the style is that of the transition period from 'strict' to 'free'. The Fantasy may be said to be one of the precursors of the Fugue. Gibbons wrote a set of nine in three parts. Other composers were R. White, Morley, Bull (Doric Fancies), and Este. C. Simpson in his *Compendium* (1665) thus describes the Fancy: 'In this sort of music the Composer (being not limited to words) doth imploy all his art and invention solely about the bringing in and carrying on of these Fuges according to the order and method formerly shewed. When he has tryed all the several ways which he thinks fit to be used therein, he takes some other point and does the like with it: or else, for variety introduces some chromatick notes, with bindings and inter-mixture of discords: or falls into some lighter humour like a Madrigal, or what else his own fancy shall lead him to: but still concluding with something which hath art and excellency in it.'

Modern Phantasies are of a much more extended nature. The following may be studied:—

H. W. Warner.   Folk Song Fantasies.   Stainer & Bell.

H. Howells.   Folk Song Fantasies.   Stainer & Bell.

R. Vaughan Williams.   Phantasy Quintet.   Stainer & Bell.

E. Goosens.   Phantasy Quartet.   J. & W. Chester.

The opening of the eighth of Gibbons's Fantasies may be quoted:—

Ex. 6.

&c.

If asked to write a Fantasy for Strings on the following tune :—

Ex. 7.

the student should not use the material in long notes ; he should use the C.F. in some form of diminution.

Ex. 8.

Then

or else elaborate it into a florid figure :—

Ex. 9.

If, however, a tune in shorter notes be given, it may be taken much as it stands.

Ex. 10.

8. *The working of problems in modulation, the opening bars being given.*

The forms will be Binary. The first half should not end on the flat side of the Tonic, and more modulation can be used in the second half than in the first. The following problem illustrates this:—

Problem.

Begin as follows:—

Third Mus. B. Oxon., May, 1903.

and modulate to D minor, B flat, G flat, D flat, and back to F.

Third Mus. B. Oxon., May, 1903.

We now have an example in triple time. Begin as follows, and modulate to D min., B flat maj., G min., C maj., and back to F.

First Mus. B. Oxon., Nov., 1900.

The working of the problem :—

Problem.

Begin as follows and modulate to B min., E min., F♯ min.,
A maj., F maj., D min., B flat maj., D maj., B min., D major.

Third Mus. B. Oxon., Nov., 1902.

If the course of the opening (D maj., B min., E min.) be
compared with the ending (D maj., B min., D maj.) it will be
seen that it is intended that the last few bars should be a recapitu-
lation of the opening, with the modulation turned so as to end in
the Tonic, after the manner of Corelli, Scarlatti, Bach, and
Handel (see Grove, Article on Form).

The working of the problem :—

Cf. bar 1.

Problem.

Begin as follows, and modulate to D maj., F♯ min., F♯ maj.,
G min., E flat maj., D maj., E min., and back to B min.

Scherzando

Mus. D. Oxon., 1903.

EXERCISES

1. Write two- and three-part Inventions on the following subjects as for pianoforte :—

(a)

&c.

(b)

&c.

(c)

&c.

(d)

&c.

2. Write an Allemande on the following Subject (3 parts) as for pianoforte :—

3. Write a two-part Gigue on the following as for pianoforte :—

4. Write a Fantasy for Violin, Viola, and 'Cello on the following material :—

5. Write Choral Preludes for the Organ on tunes of your own choice, and according to the various methods explained.

Printed in England at the Oxford University Press